FROM TIME TO ETERNITY

THE JOURNEY TO HEAVEN

FROM TIME TO ETERNITY

THE JOURNEY TO HEAVEN

JOHN FLADER

CONNOR COURT PUBLISHING PTY LTD

Published in 2024 by Connor Court Publishing Pty Ltd

Copyright © John Flader 2024

ALL RIGHTS RESERVED. No part of this book may be reproduced or transmitted in any form or by any means, electronic or mechanical, including photocopying, recording, or by any information storage and retrieval system without express written permission from the publisher.

Connor court Publishing Pty Ltd
PO Box 7257
Redland Bay QLD 4165
sales@connorcourt.com
www.connorcourt.com

ISBN: 9781923224252

Bible citations from The Revised Standard Version.

Cover design by Mathew De Sousa
Photo credit: (Eternity image) Sardaka, CC BY-SA 3.0

Printed in Australia

Dedicated to all those who will read this book and be helped by it to share eternity with God in heaven.

Contents

Foreword	1
Introduction	7
1. Getting started	13
2. The destination is real	21
The soul	21
Near-death experiences	24
People who have come back from the dead	29
3. The destination is attractive	35
Heaven	36
Hell	43
Our goal in life	48
4. The God who awaits us	51
God is love	52
God is mercy	54
God is Father	57
God is provident	60
We will meet Jesus too	63
5. Talking with God in prayer	65
Vocal prayers	65
The psalms	66
The Lord's Prayer	67
The Hail Mary	68
The rosary	68
Meditation	71

Difficulties in prayer	72
Finding our own way	78
6. HEART IN GOD, NOT IN GOODS	79
Getting our priorities right	79
Detachment of the heart	82
The dangers of love of wealth	83
Another way of life	84
Generosity with our wealth	86
7. STRIVING TO PLEASE GOD	91
Listening to our conscience	92
Other voices	93
The jigsaw puzzle of life	94
8. GROWING IN VIRTUES	97
Prudence	98
Justice	99
Fortitude	99
Temperance	100
9. OBSTACLES ALONG THE WAY	103
The world	104
The flesh	106
The devil	115
10. ENCOURAGING OTHERS TO GO WITH US	119
Concern for others' spiritual health	119
Everyone is looking for God	120
Example and word	121
Instruments of God	123

11. Sporting spirit — 125
    Having a goal — 125
    Striving for the goal — 126
    Sacrifice and self-control — 128
    A training program — 130
    The coach — 132
    Coping with failures — 134
    The doctor or physiotherapist — 136
    Following the rules — 137
    Time-outs — 138
    Finishing the race — 139

Foreword

In his new book, *From Time to Eternity*, John Flader provides a valuable follow-up to his previous works on life after death, *Dying to Live – Reflections on life after death* and *The Final Exam – Preparing for the Judgment*. The author shares here his aspirations, rich experiences, and profound understanding of eternity, offering, as it were, a guidebook for contemplating and preparing for eternal life with God.

To situate the book in its context, the author reminds the reader of some of the ideas from Dying to Live, skilfully summarising Dr Raymond Moody's work on thousands of documented near-death experiences, which offer a glimpse of life after death. He also shows evidence for life after death from apparitions on earth of persons who have died and are now enjoying eternal life with God. He makes clear that eternal life is accessible to everyone, no matter what their religion. The book will fill readers with joy and enthusiasm to live in such a way as to achieve eternal life with God.

In my many years of practising psychology, I have seen how people's perception of eternal life has a great bearing on how they answer three fundamental questions: 1) Who am I? (Being), 2) How and where do I find love? (Relating), and 3) Who will I become, or how do I help myself to be loved and to love? (Becoming). I have found that existential anxiety often arises from an inability to find the meaning of life, leading to a sense of the inevitability of loneliness and death, and the fear of the unknown. At the same time, I have seen many patients whose lives were completely turned around when they discovered the true meaning of life and the awareness of a God who loves them and whom they can love in return.

Many alcoholics, for example, have been greatly helped by reciting the Serenity Prayer used in Alcoholics Anonymous: "God, grant me the serenity to accept the things I cannot change, the courage to change the things I can, and the wisdom to know the difference." When these people have entered into a personal relationship with God through prayer, they have seen their levels of stress, anxiety, and depression greatly reduced. They were helped to focus on the present moment, giving them inner peace. I am confident that From Time to Eternity, in its description of a God of love and mercy who has a place in heaven for everyone, and in its emphasis on prayer, will help many people follow this way.

To give an example, one patient with no religious background started on this journey and found great peace when he picked up a card with a prayer which he began to say regularly. It read:

> Jesus Christ, I do not know you well enough. Reveal yourself to me if you are the living God who sees and hears me. I ask you to forgive all my sins and cover me with your precious blood. Send forth your spirit to correct, enlighten, and deliver me from all evils and deceptions. Help me to be your beloved disciple and to follow your way of love all the days of my life. Thank you for the love you give me as I draw close to you now. In the name of Jesus Christ, I pray. Amen.

This patient later joined a church group and became a committed Catholic. He died of a heart attack in his mid-70s but, two weeks before he died, he gave his therapist a book with this prayer:

> Holy Spirit, thank you for stirring in me and giving me the noble desire to seek the Father's will, granting me the wisdom to understand his will, the humility to accept his will, the courage to do his will, the strength to persevere in following his will, the patience to maintain effort in fulfilling his will, and the love of Christ to love the Father's will. Father, I rely daily on your bread of love and transformative grace so that I can continuously seek, understand, accept, do, follow, fulfill, and love your will. Your divine will for me is to love others as much as you love me. Father, only your love can shape my life until I reach eternity to love you as you deserve. In Jesus' name, I pray. Amen.

He had a radical transformation when he found the answers to the three fundamental questions. He realised that he was a child of God, who loved him and had a place for him in heaven. He had found God, who is love, who is mercy, and who is a Father. I believe there are many people like him who will be helped by *From Time to Eternity*, which speaks powerfully about God and man's relationship with him. In showing how heaven is a state of indescribable love, peace and joy, free from all suffering, the book fills readers with hope for eternal life, enhancing their quality of life and giving them a sense of purpose and direction. They are encouraged and helped throughout the book to live a virtuous life in preparation for the afterlife. They will find in this book many profound insights and thought-provoking reflections that will challenge them to expand their perspective, question their assumptions, and explore new understandings of eternity.

All of this is consistent with empirical studies in positive psychology, which align with psychiatrist Victor Frankl's logotherapy, showing how a sense of purpose in life along with ethical behaviour acts as a buffer against existential voids and psychological distress. People with a growing sense of meaning in life report lower levels of anxiety, depression, and stress. They also have higher levels of happiness, life satisfaction, and overall well-being.

I am convinced that this book will be a valuable resource for those seeking answers to life's deepest questions and desiring a closer relationship with God. The author highlights the communal aspect of heaven, which can be particularly comforting. It reinforces the idea that relationships and love extend beyond earthly existence, nurturing a sense of continuity and connection that alleviates existential loneliness.

From Time to Eternity thus constitutes a handbook for understanding and embracing the concept of eternity. Its many stories, documented accounts, and practical wisdom on prayer and virtuous living will help readers keep their eye on the goal of eternal life with God and avoid the pitfalls that would draw their attention away from that goal. The book serves as a beacon of hope, reminding readers that eternal life is not mere wishful thinking, a vague fantasy, or a distant promise; it is a present reality that can transform lives in the here and now.

I wholeheartedly endorse this book and encourage readers to approach it with an attitude of reverence and humility, recognising that the mysteries of life and eternity are vast and unfathomable. As they embark on this journey of self-discovery and spiritual exploration, they should set aside preconceptions and adopt a spirit of curiosity and openness. Readers will find here profound wisdom and timeless truths that can transform their lives and awaken their desire for what truly matters. They will be guided to delve into the mysteries of existence and to discover the deeper meaning of life, death, and eternity.

John Poon, BSc, DCH, MASH, MANA, MAPS
Retired Health Psychologist
President of the Australian Society of Hypnosis, NSW (2019-2024)

Introduction

In November 1932, a 47-year-old Sydney man named Arthur Stace, who had grown up in abject poverty, became an alcoholic in his teens, went to jail at 15 for drunkenness and was illiterate, attended a sermon in a Baptist church on the topic "Echoes of Eternity". The preacher, John Ridley, said: "Eternity, eternity, I wish that I could sound or shout that word to everyone in the streets of Sydney. You've got to meet it; where will you spend eternity?" The words so captivated Stace that he immediately took a piece of chalk out of his pocket, bent down and wrote the word "Eternity" on the church floor. Even though he could hardly write his own name legibly, the word came out in beautiful handwriting in a way that not even Stace could understand.

From then on, until his death in 1967, Stace would rise early in the morning every day and write "Eternity" in yellow chalk all over Sydney's footpaths. Only in 1956 did someone see him and discover who the graffiti artist was. So famous did the graffiti become that the word "Eternity" was emblazoned in lights on the Sydney Harbour Bridge for the New Year's Eve fireworks at the turn of the millennium in 2000. It was also used later that year in the opening ceremony of the Sydney Olympic Games.

Thanks to Stace, Sydney was reminded of eternity every day for 35 years, and the world was reminded of it in 2000. But the years have passed and now many people are quite unaware of it. In 1932 John Ridley, the Baptist preacher, wished he could shout the word to everyone in Sydney and ask them, "Where will you spend eternity?" Today, when there is more need than ever, there are few voices like his. Many people, perhaps the majority, are completely unaware of the eternal life that awaits them when they die. Or they know it but do nothing about it.

That is why I wrote this book. It proposes to remind the reader that eternal life is a reality and to offer advice on how to prepare for it. It is a reality for everyone. The question is: "Where will you spend it?" Will it be in indescribable happiness with God forever in heaven, or in the indescribable suffering of separation from God in hell?

The question is important. Very important. It concerns the very purpose of our life on earth. We live here for a short time, even though it may be a hundred years, in order to prepare for eternal life with God. If we miss out on heaven, our life will have been a total failure.

For many people, perhaps most, this question does not enter their thoughts as they go about their daily life. Even if they know there is eternal life after life here on earth, they don't give it the importance it deserves.

Fourteen centuries ago, Pope St Gregory the Great urged people to pursue single-mindedly the goal of eternal life with God in heaven. His words are still relevant today:

> So our Lord's sheep will finally reach their grazing ground where all who follow him in simplicity of heart will feed on the green pastures of eternity. These pastures are the spiritual joys of heaven. There the elect look upon the face of God with unclouded vision and feast at the banquet of life for ever more.
>
> Beloved brothers, let us set out for these pastures where we shall keep joyful festival with so many of our fellow

citizens. May the thought of their happiness urge us on! Let us stir up our hearts, rekindle our faith, and long eagerly for what heaven has in store for us. To love thus is to be already on our way. No matter what obstacles we encounter, we must not allow them to turn us aside from the joy of that heavenly feast. Anyone who is determined to reach his destination is not deterred by the roughness of the road that leads to it. Nor must we allow the charm of success to seduce us, or we shall be like a foolish traveler who is so distracted by the pleasant meadows through which he is passing that he forgets where he is going (*Homily on the Gospels* 14, 3-6).

This book is a logical sequel to its predecessors, *Dying to live – Reflections on life after death* and *The Final Exam – Preparing for the judgment*. The first book showed the reader that there is indeed life after death, whether one believes in it or not, and it went on to describe the Christian understanding of that life. The second book was a reflection on moral life, to help the reader know what is right and wrong and thus guide him on the road to eternity. It spoke about the objective nature of morality, the role of conscience and the importance of the virtues, before going on to consider particular moral issues. All of this was based, not on the Bible but on the natural law.

The present book proposes practical ways to help the reader keep the goal of eternal life in mind on a daily basis. It begins by calling to mind some of the key ideas of Dying to Live, including the reality of life after death and the nature of that life, so as to make clear what the goal of life is. It then deals with what we know about the loving, merciful God who awaits us in heaven, and how we can establish a personal relationship with him here on earth.

Since we naturally tend to be absorbed by the world and its many attractions, the next chapter shows how to be detached from the world and to put our heart in God, not in goods, when we live in a materialistic society which we are called to make more human.

Then comes a chapter on striving to please God throughout the day by doing what we understand to be his will for us in every moment. Since this is not always easy, the following chapter deals with the importance of growing in the traditional virtues of prudence, justice, fortitude and temperance. And lest we be naïve and think that our moral life is meant to be a walk in the park, the next chapter warns of the obvious obstacles we will face along the way, considered as the world, the flesh and the devil.

As we make our way through life, if we care about those around us, we will want to help them too follow the path that leads to heaven. The book explains the importance of doing this and it offers suggestions about how to go about it.

Finally, the last chapter compares our efforts to live a good life with those of a sportsperson who wants to excel, showing the many parallels between the sporting life and the spiritual life. It encourages us to adopt a sporting spirit in our spiritual life.

Like its predecessors, *From Time to Eternity* is addressed to people of all religious beliefs and of none. After all, eternity is for everyone. The book makes frequent reference to the teachings of Jesus Christ. No matter what one's religion, Christ is universally acknowledged as a great moral teacher. But, as we have seen in *Dying to Live*, in addition to being a great moral teacher, Christ not only claimed to be, but showed by his life that he was God, God in the flesh. It makes eminent sense to listen to what he has to say.

It is my hope that many will benefit from this book, and that it will help them keep the destination in mind as they go about their daily life, so as to prepare well to receive the eternal reward God has in store for them.

As a final note, C.S. Lewis, in his *Mere Christianity*, sums up perfectly what this book is about:

> I must keep alive in myself the desire for my true country, which I shall not find till after death; I must never let it get snowed under or turned aside; I must make it the main object of life to press on to that other country and to help others to do the same.

1

Getting started

Your alarm goes off. 6.30. What day is it? Thursday. What's on today? Same as yesterday. And tomorrow. Go to work. Get out of bed, shower and shave, help your wife feed the kids breakfast. Help prepare their lunches. Leave home at 7.30, catch the 7.47 train.

Arrive at work. Anything special on today? Just a meeting at 11, but you've prepared your report, and the meeting goes well.

Leave the office around 5.30, catch the 5.49 train. Arrive home at 6.30. Have dinner with the family. Chat for a while at the table, catching up on what has happened with the kids at school and with your wife. Help your wife clean up. Put the kids to bed. Relax for a while with the newspaper or TV, chat with your wife. Go to bed around 10.30. Same as usual on most weekdays. All organised.

What's on this weekend? Work around the house Saturday morning, mow the lawn, maybe wash the car. Often drive the kids to sport and watch their game. Your son's only 11 but already he's a pretty good soccer player, and he really likes you to watch him play.

Relax a bit in the afternoon, watch a film on TV with the family in the evening. Same as most Saturdays. It's a family routine. Everyone loves it.

Outing with the family on Sunday. Going to the zoo this weekend. The kids love it. And you like it too. Help your wife prepare the lunches, leave around 10.30 and spend most of the day there, returning around 4 in the afternoon. A great day.

Any holidays planned in the next few months? Yes, you're going to the place on the lake where you go every year during the Easter break. Nice place. Chance to go boating and swimming, even fishing. The kids love it. You book it every year for the following year so it's all organised.

Any bigger events planned for this year? Yes, you're going to Italy for your niece's wedding in July. You have relatives there and the kids can play with their cousins. They love it. They're even learning a little Italian, your ancestral language. You're staying for two weeks with your brother and his family. You'll travel around that part of Italy for a few days. Very pleasant. You've been there before. Booked the tickets several months ago. All organised.

How about next year during the summer break? You're thinking about it, but haven't decided yet. Sometimes you go to the place on the lake, but you're considering going on a cruise next year. Very cheap holiday, you know. For one price you get your travel to different destinations, your accommodation, your meals and even lots of entertainment. You've done this before with friends and their children. Everyone enjoys it. It's still over a year away but you'll check with your friends and probably make a booking soon. You get a better price when you book in advance.

So, as is obvious, you're well organised. Everything planned in advance. No last-minute hassles or worries. Well done.

But how about that other journey, to that other destination, the most important one, when all is said and done?

What do you mean?

I mean when you die.

When you die? It's all over then, isn't it? You don't have to worry about that. Someone else will look after your funeral. You've made your will so it's all organised. Just live your life and enjoy it, and when your time is up, it's up. You can't control that. Better not even to think about it. Don't be morbid. Do your best, do what you think is right, and get on with life. It's about life, not about death. Make the best of it while you're still here.

Are you certain about that – that it's all over? That there's no life after death? No heaven forever with God? And, of course, no hell either? Maybe, you think, it's safer to say no to both, just in case there might be a hell.

But the existence or not of life after death may not depend on what you think about it. There might just be reality out there, independently of what you think. The way you talk, you're betting there isn't a heaven or a hell. It's all over when you die. Okay, but what if you're wrong?

Let me tell you a true story from my book *Dying to Live* – reflections on life after death. It's about a 24-year-old New Zealand surfer named Ian McCormack, who didn't believe in life after death either. Until he came face to face with death. He describes himself as an atheist, as well as a gambler, and he was living "the good life" when he suddenly found himself at death's door.

On a trip around South-East Asia, McCormack was diving for seafood one night off the coast of Mauritius, when he felt a strong stinging on his arm. He discovered that he had been stung by a box jellyfish, and by the time he got out of the water he had been stung five times. He knew those jellyfish can kill a person in ten to fifteen minutes. His arm quickly swelled to twice its size and he was becoming progressively paralysed and drowsy. He says: "I was dying. If I don't make it and die before I get to the hospital, what would happen to me? Is there life after death, or when a man dies, is that it? Finished. Cessation of life. Well, as a heathen, as an atheist, I reckoned when you died it was all over. The trouble was, I wasn't sure. You can be wrong. I was a gambler and I'm gambling with my life here. If I'm gambling and I'm wrong here, I'm gambling; it's like Russian roulette. I could be wrong here. I have no idea what would happen to me if I died."

On his way to the hospital in an ambulance he somehow saw his mother praying for him. She was the only one in the family who prayed, he says. He also saw the words of the Lord's Prayer, "Forgive us our trespasses". It moved him to beg God to forgive his many sins. Upon arrival at the hospital, he passed out and appeared to have died, remaining unconscious for some fifteen minutes.

During that time his soul left the body and went first to hell, which he realised he would have deserved had he not begged God to forgive his sins. Then he experienced heaven, with its unimaginable joy, such that he would have preferred not to return to life on earth. But then he considered that if he remained in heaven, his mother would spend the rest of her life worrying that her son had gone to hell, such was the immoral life he was living. He knew he had to return. And, in any case, his time wasn't up, and his soul returned to the body. He regained consciousness, much to the amazement of the hospital staff, who thought he was dead. He returned to New Zealand and discovered that his mother had been praying for him at the very time he was dying. As can be imagined, the experience changed his life forever. For the better. He now knew for certain that there is life after death.

We can learn a lot from his experience. Many people, like him, in the fulness of youth and health, are quite happy to put off the question of life after death, and they even deny its existence. But when they suddenly come face to face with death, they take it seriously. Because there is a lot at stake. Ian McCormack realised that what would happen to him if he died did not depend on what he, as an atheist, thought might happen. There was reality, independent of what he thought. There was life after death, and he was not prepared for it.

In that critical moment, he articulated what has come to be known as Pascal's wager. Let me summarise what I wrote about it in *Dying to Live*. In the seventeenth century, Blaise Pascal (1623-1662), the famous French mathematician, physicist, inventor and philosopher, posed the question of the bet we are considering. He was writing for the sceptics of his own day to help them consider the possibilities – and the consequences – of the wager that there is, or there is not, a God and, with God, life after death. His argument comes in his Pensées, or Thoughts. His argument is well worth considering. A summary of it goes like this.

Either there is a God – and life after death – or there isn't. Pascal says that reason cannot decide between the two. He says this because he is writing for sceptics, who think that by reason alone one cannot know whether there is a God. Actually, human reason can know with certainty that there is a God. I dedicate a whole chapter to it in *Dying to Live*, arguing from scientific findings about the universe in the twentieth century, some of which have convinced atheists. But let us continue with Pascal.

Human life is like a game, in which in the end there is a God and life after death or there isn't. It's like tossing a coin, which will come up heads or tails. Heads means there is a God and, if you have lived and died well, you live happily ever after with him in indescribable bliss. That's heaven. Or, if not, you might find yourself in everlasting suffering in hell. Tails means there is no God and your life just comes to an end. You must place a bet, you must decide how you are going to live. It's not optional. That is, you are going to die sooner or later and you will find out then whether it was heads or tails. But then it's too late. And you have to live with the consequences of your choice.

In fact, we could add, people do wager. Everyone does, whether they think so or not. Many believe in God and strive to live in accordance with that belief, making an effort to live a good moral life. Others believe there is no God and they don't worry about morality or about what happens when they die. They will just cease to exist, so they think – and hope. Some of these people, nonetheless, "hedge their bets" and endeavour to live a decent life "just in case".

Let us first consider the consequences if we bet that there is a God and life after death, and so we strive to live a good life. If we win and there is a God, we gain everything. We bet the short life we live on earth, trying to live it well, and we gain union with God for all eternity in heaven. If we lose and there is no God, we haven't lost anything. We simply cease to exist after living a good life here on earth, with all its joys and satisfaction. So, betting on God offers the chance to gain everything and lose nothing.

Or we can bet that there is no God, no life after death, that when we die, that's it – we simply cease to exist. It's all over. Then, as many who do not believe in God will do, we may fall more readily into self-indulgence, self-centredness, dishonesty, pride, laziness, etc. If we win and there is no God, we gain nothing, because there is nothing to gain. There is no life after death. But if we lose and there is a God and life after death, we miss out on the reward of eternal happiness with him in heaven. We lose everything. Everything. And of course, although Pascal doesn't say it, this can also mean we end up suffering for all eternity in hell. Yes, hell. It exists, whether we believe in it or not. So there's a lot at stake.

All of this suggests something very important. Just as you are well organised in your day-to-day, even year-to-year, earthly plans, you should apply the same seriousness to the most important plan of all – the journey of life. The journey to eternal life. The journey to heaven. There's a lot at stake. Everything. Eternity.

But how do you prepare for this? First, convince yourself that life after death is real. That is the topic of the next chapter.

2

THE DESTINATION IS REAL

When you are preparing for a trip, the first step is to choose the destination and be convinced that there is a good reason for going there. That is the easy part. You may have been there before, or you have read about it and it looks attractive, or friends may have been there and have encouraged you to try it out too. If you are sold on the idea, you start making plans. But if you are still uncertain, you probably won't bother.

You can naturally apply the same reasoning to the journey of life, the journey to heaven. If you are not convinced that the destination is real, or attractive, you will put it on the back burner. You are not going to do anything about it for the time being. Maybe in the future. Maybe never. Bad choice.

I wrote my book *Dying to Live* to show that life after death is real. I wrote it especially for people who don't believe in it. The best way to convince yourself, if you are not already convinced, would be to get that book and read it. But, to save you time, here I will pass on some of the key ideas.

The soul

One of the key pointers to life after death is the existence in human beings of a spiritual soul. What do we mean by a soul? In general, a soul is the life principle of any living being. It is what distinguishes a living thing from a non-living one. Rocks, soil, water, atoms don't have souls. Plants, animals and humans do. It is the soul which gives life, unity to the living thing, making it function as a single entity.

For example, in the case of a living plant, all of its parts – the roots, stem, leaves, flowers – work together to keep the plant alive, growing and able to reproduce itself. But because the plant soul – or the animal soul, for that matter – is not spiritual, when the plant dies, the soul, the organising principle, ceases to exist and the various parts of the plant decay and disintegrate. The plant decomposes into the elements that made it up. The Greek philosopher Aristotle (384-322 BC) called the plant soul *bios*, from which we get the word biology.

In the case of animals, which are of a higher order than plants, the growth and reproductive functions of plants are there, but in addition the animal has the ability to move and to experience sensations. Aristotle called the animal soul *zoê*, from which we get the word zoology. The animal soul, or sensitive soul, includes the functions of the vegetative or plant soul. But since the animal soul, like the plant soul, is not spiritual – it is just the unifying, organising principle of the animal – when the animal dies the soul ceases to exist and the animal decays and breaks up into its constituent elements. The animal simply is no more.

But when we come to humans, we find something completely different. In addition to the functions of reproduction and growth in plants, and those of movement and sensation in animals, humans have the ability to think, to plan, to reason. These are spiritual functions, in some way independent of matter. Aristotle called the human soul the psūchê, the psyche, from which we get the word psychology.

By its spiritual soul, the human person is radically different from animals, including the highest apes. A person can think of a better way to do things, and so make progress over time. Humans invented a way to make fire, spears, bows and arrows, boomerangs, wheels, carts, internal combustion engines, motor vehicles, airplanes, rockets, and space craft capable of flying to the moon and back. Humans found ways to plant seeds and grow crops, cure illnesses with medicines, and make radios, television sets and computers. They developed language, and produced works of art, literature and music. Animals can't do this. They do not have a spiritual soul which allows them to think or reason. They simply live the way they always have, following their instincts. Birds always make their nests in the same way, spiders make their webs in the same way, chimpanzees mate and raise their offspring in the same way … In a word, they do not make progress.

Yes, higher animals like dogs and especially apes, have what we can call the affective life: the emotions, the feelings. They show affection for their young, they play with one another, they appear to be happy or sad, angry or frightened. In this they can sometimes appear to be almost human. Since the human soul includes the functions of the vegetative soul of plants and the sensitive soul of animals, the human person has the affective life in common with these lower beings. But that does not make animals human. It simply means that they have some functions in common with us and we humans have some functions in common with them.

Humans are radically different from the highest animals because our soul is spiritual. In addition to knowing material objects like food, cars and books, we humans can know and think about completely immaterial objects, like goodness, love, honesty and truth. A material being like a plant or animal cannot do that. Yes, we have a brain, as do animals, through which we know and think, but our soul is in some way independent of the brain, of a higher order than it, allowing us to understand and think about the immaterial, the spiritual. A material organ like the brain cannot by itself know something spiritual like goodness and love. And it cannot know that it knows, reflect on its own actions, as we humans can.

The importance of all of this is that a spiritual soul, because it is spiritual, cannot be destroyed when we die. Spirit has no matter to be destroyed. It of necessity lives on. How or where it lives on we know from other sources, but of necessity it lives on. In fact, death is traditionally defined as the separation of the soul from the body.

So yes, we have a spiritual soul, distinct from the body, and it continues to exist in a conscious state when we die. It doesn't just fade away into nothingness. It doesn't cease to exist. There is life after death, whether we believe in it or not.

Near-death experiences

If you want more evidence for the separate existence of the soul, you can look at the numerous accounts of near-death experiences, where a person has suffered severe trauma, like a cardiac arrest, and is clinically dead before being resuscitated. During this time thousands of people have related later how their soul separated from the body and was watching its own resuscitation.

In one such case a man who had been in a deep coma and his soul had left the body, later told a nurse that he recognised her and, when she was looking for his dentures, he told her where she had put them while he was unconscious. They were there, precisely where he said. In another case an elderly woman who had suffered a cardiac arrest felt her soul leave the body, hover above it, and observe the resuscitation. After she was revived, she told one of the doctors how she had seen his pen fall from his pocket and how he had gone over to pick it up near the window, where her soul was watching. The doctor was amazed. What is more, and truly extraordinary, is that the woman was blind, but now, with her soul outside the body, she could see.

There are literally thousands of documented accounts of near-death experiences (NDEs) and many books and articles have been written about them. Some of the books have been bestsellers. NDEs are as real as the life experiences we all have. I personally have known at least four people who have had them. My doctor friends too say they have known people who have had them. NDEs are worthy of consideration and we can learn a lot from them.

Across the thousands of people who have had NDEs, there are some common elements. The first is the soul leaving the body and hovering above it, fully aware of what is happening below, even though the person is unconscious. The person later recounts details of what they saw in the efforts to resuscitate them. A second stage, experienced by many, involves the soul going through a tunnel towards a bright light, where they experience great love, peace and joy. They recognise this as heaven. Some in that state are aware of a divine being bathed in light, and many see loved ones who have preceded them in death.

Many describe seeing their whole life flash by in an instant, including the effect their actions have had on others. This phenomenon which has come to be called the life review. Some experience hell, and others a place of purification known as purgatory. When their soul returns to the body and they regain consciousness, they often say that in that state they were more alive than ever before. They are spiritually transformed and they invariably change their life for the better. The experience convinces them that what we know as death is just a passing into another realm of existence. They lose their fear of dying and feel more joy in this life.

The description of these experiences is remarkably similar among all who have had them, no matter what prior religious belief they may have had. They may have had a strong belief in some religion or absolutely none, they may have lived a good life or been a big sinner, been an adult or a young child. It doesn't make any difference. They all have similar experiences.

One researcher into NDEs is Dr Jeffrey Long, who has written several books about them, including the *New York Times* bestseller *Evidence of the Afterlife*. Dr Long has found that the great majority of those experiencing an NDE, when given a choice, do not want to return to their body and to life on earth. The reason is that they feel very intense positive emotions in their near-death experience, indescribable happiness, more so than they ever knew on earth. They greatly enjoy this experience, which many call heaven, and they have a sense of familiarity as if they have been there before. They very much want to stay and not return to earth.

In his most recent survey of people with NDEs, Dr Long asked whether the person encountered any awareness that God, or a supreme being, either exists or does not exist. He was astounded to find that virtually all, with one exception out of hundreds, answered yes, that they experienced an awareness of God, or encountered him directly. What is more, they never described God as judgmental, angry or wrathful. Rather they found an overwhelmingly loving presence, which gave them a great sense of peace. They often experienced a union, a oneness with God, and many had a conversation with him.

When asked whether they received any information regarding

the purpose and meaning of life on earth, a common response was yes, that we are truly spiritual beings who have an earthly existence, but our real nature is called to something beyond this life. We are on earth to learn lessons on how to live, how to love and be united with others, in order to prepare ourselves for the next life, where we really belong, where we will have a loving existence and be truly happy.

Dr Long is convinced by his research that what we call the soul is clearly distinct from the body and the brain. He says: "It's just that there's some other part of us that seems to be intimately related to our consciousness and who we are, and what we are, that's much more than our physical brain. And it's non-physical clearly. Some call it the soul, but the term to use is neither here nor there. Every shred of evidence from near-death experiences and a number of other related experiences all convincingly point to the conclusion that consciousness, that critical part of who we are, survives physical brain death."

Another person to write extensively on NDEs, and indeed the first, is Dr Raymond A. Moody, a psychiatrist whose book *Life After Life* (1975) was a bestseller. In *The Light Beyond* (Rider, UK, 2005), a revised and updated edition of that book, he says that the near-death experience changes the person's life for the better, and he identifies eight aspects of these changes.

First, these persons no longer fear death, even if they have lived a good part of their life fearing it. They are convinced that what we know as death is merely a passing to another state of existence. They realised that the "being of light", God, loves and cares for them, that he is not judgmental, but rather wants them to develop into better people. Instead of living in fear, they focus on becoming more loving people.

Second, they sense the importance of love and almost all say that love is now the most important thing in their life. They usually feel much more joy in this life and they are convinced that there is a purpose to this life, which is to learn to love one another.

Third, they have a sense of greater connection with all things, including the world of nature.

Fourth, they acquire a greater appreciation for learning and a new thirst for knowledge. This is not knowledge for knowledge's sake but rather knowledge that contributes to being a more whole, complete person.

Fifth, they have a new feeling of control, of responsibility for the course of their lives. Having had the life review, they are more sensitive to the immediate and long-term consequences of their actions.

Sixth, they have a greater sense of urgency, of the shortness and fragility of their lives. It helps them see that their life is precious, that it is the little things that matter, that they have to live their life to the full.

Seventh, they have a new awareness of the spiritual side of life. Many are led to study and accept the spiritual teachings of the great religious thinkers. Dr Moody says that even people who didn't believe in God before, come to believe in him after an NDE.

Eighth, after experiencing a spiritual paradise, they have difficulty in re-entering and adjusting to the real world.

Dr Moody has interviewed many children who have had NDEs and he finds that their experiences are similar to those of adults. He concludes that the experiences of children give better evidence for life after death than those of older people, because older people have had more time to be influenced by their life's experiences and their religious beliefs, whereas children come with a certain freshness. Dr Moody concludes, after over thirty years of studying NDEs, that those who have these experiences do get a glimpse of the life beyond, a brief passage into a whole other state of reality.

These NDEs on their own can be a big help in assuring us of the separate existence of the soul, of the existence of life after death, of the true meaning of life and how to live it to the full. We don't have to have a near-death experience ourselves to be convinced of this. We can take others' word for it.

People who have come back from the dead

Much rarer than near-death experiences are the cases of people who have lived on earth, have died and have come back from the dead. What, you say, come back from the dead? Yes, back from the dead.

The most obvious and well-known of these is Jesus Christ, who died on a cross outside of Jerusalem two thousand years ago and then rose from the dead and appeared numerous times in his body over the next forty days before ascending into heaven. There is no question but that all this happened in history. If Jesus had not risen from the dead, I can assure you that his disciples would have gone back to their fishing and tax collecting within weeks of his death. Instead, they went all over and spread faith in Christ, dying for their faith as martyrs. If Christ had not come back from the dead, the Church he founded would have died out in the first century, yet it is still here and it is in fact the largest single religion in the world today. Yes, Christ came back from the dead to die no more. It has made all the difference.

Another person who has come back from the dead and appeared on earth numerous times over the centuries is Mary, the mother of Jesus. Let us consider just one of these cases, her apparitions in Fatima, Portugal, in 1917. What happened at Fatima had extraordinary consequences and left no doubt that Mary actually came back from the next life.

Mary appeared to three small children, aged 10, 9 and 7, each month from May through October, 1917. In the July apparition she made a prophecy that was borne out several months later, telling the children that on October 13 she would work a miracle that would be seen by everyone.

On October 13 some 70,000 people trudged through the rain and mud in the hope of seeing the miracle. Although it had been raining steadily, suddenly the clouds parted and the sun appeared. It began to revolve, sending out rays of light of different colours that lit up the surroundings, and then it seemed to fall towards the earth. The people fell on their knees and begged God for mercy and, to their great relief, the sun returned to its place. All those present and even some in the surrounding villages saw the miracle. Sceptics reported seeing it and the anti-clerical newspapers in Lisbon had articles about it. The fulfilment of the prophecy in such a dramatic way can only be explained if Mary did in fact come back to earth to prophesy the miracle.

That is not the only prediction Mary made in the July apparition that was later borne out. She also told the children: "This war [the First World War (1914-1918), then in progress] will end, but if men do not refrain from offending God, another and more terrible war will begin during the pontificate of Pius XI. When you see a night that is lit by a strange and unknown light you will know it is the sign God gives you that he is about to punish the world with war..." Here Mary made three more predictions.

First, there would be another terrible war which was, of course, the Second World War.

Second, the war would be preceded by a "strange and unknown light". On the night of 25-26 January 1938, an exceedingly bright light, the Aurora Borealis or Northern Lights, was seen over a large part of Western Europe, as far south as Spain and Portugal. It was so exceptional that newspapers reported it. An article in the *New York Times* on 26 January read: "The Aurora Borealis, rarely seen in Southern or Western Europe, spread fear in parts of Portugal and lower Austria tonight while thousands of Britons were brought running into the streets in wonderment. The ruddy glow led many to think half the city was ablaze … The lights were clearly seen in Italy, Spain and even Gibraltar… Portuguese villagers rushed in fright from their homes, fearing the end of the world."

The third prediction was that the war would begin when Pius XI was Pope. In 1917, when Mary appeared at Fatima, the Pope was Benedict XV, who was to die in January 1922. The new Pope, chosen on February 6 that year, could have taken any name he wished, but in fact he chose the name Pius XI. While the Second World War began, strictly speaking, with Hitler's invasion of Poland on 1 September 1939, when the Pope was Pius XII, it could be said that it began when Hitler annexed Austria and made claims over parts of the Czech Republic in 1938, during the reign of Pius XI.

There is no way to explain what happened at Fatima and afterwards except by acknowledging that Mary, the mother of Jesus, who had lived on earth 2000 years before, did in fact come back from the next life and appeared to three children to tell them these things.

Apart from the resurrection of Christ and the numerous apparitions of Mary, there are also many books full of accounts of souls of people who have died and have later appeared on earth from that state of purification after death which is called purgatory. In these, a person who is clearly recognised, appears in a spiritual way, sometimes as if on fire, and often appeals for mercy and prayers.

One such apparition is related by St Margaret Mary Alacoque (1647-1690), a Catholic nun:

> When I was praying before the Blessed Sacrament on the feast of Corpus Christi, a person enveloped in fire suddenly stood before me. From the pitiable state the soul was in, I knew it was in purgatory and I wept bitterly. This soul told me it was that of a Benedictine, who had once heard my confession and ordered me to go to Holy Communion. As a reward for this, God permitted him to ask me to help him in his sufferings. He asked me to apply to him all I should do or suffer for a period of three months... It would be difficult for me to describe what I had to endure during those three months. He never left me and seeing him, as it were on fire and in such terrible pain, I could do nothing but groan and weep almost incessantly.

After three months of her prayers and suffering offered to God for him, the soul went to heaven.

In the twentieth century, well-known saints Padre Pio and Faustina Kowalska had visits from souls in purgatory. These few well-documented accounts, of the many hundreds in existence, again speak to us powerfully of life after death.

So, in the journey to heaven, the destination is real. The journey does not end when we die. In a real sense, it is just beginning then. When we die, we pass from our short life here on earth to an eternal existence in the next life. We can't kid ourselves about this. We can't try to convince ourselves that all this is just pious make-believe. It is real. There is life after death, whether we believe in it or not. Our journey has a real destination beyond life here on earth. If we prepare so well here for our numerous trips around the country and the world, we should prepare all the more for the most important journey of all.

Now it is time to look in greater detail at the destination to which we are going.

3

THE DESTINATION IS ATTRACTIVE

The various world religions have different perceptions of what awaits us in the next life. These religions have come from founders who lived at different times, ancient or more recent, in different parts of the world. Naturally, they have come up with different ideas of the afterlife.

What is striking, however, is that the thousands of accounts of near-death experiences of people of all religions and of none, converge on the reality of life after death as taught by Jesus Christ. As you can read in the Bible, or in a simplified form in my book *Dying to Live*, Jesus Christ was not just one more human founder of a world religion. He was truly God as well as truly man. What he said about himself and the miracles he did, including his own resurrection from the dead after being crucified, all convince us of this reality. For this reason, and because what he taught about life after death coincides with what so many people have seen in their near-death experiences, it makes sense to study his teaching about the final destination of our journey of life. For this, we will make use of the Bible and of the teachings of the Church Christ founded.

In *Dying to Live* I wrote at some length about the destination, which can be either heaven or hell, but here it will be sufficient to remind ourselves of some of the key ideas. As we have seen, we have a spiritual soul, which outlives the body and it longs for, is made for, something beyond what it can attain in this life. This longing finds its fulfilment only in heaven, and there it is truly satisfied. Here on earth, we long for happiness and we find it up to a point. But our happiness here comes and goes, and it varies in intensity. Some things give us more happiness than others. Clearly, we were made for something more, for complete happiness. We will have it in heaven.

The numerous near-death experiences, where people found themselves in a state of absolute bliss, peace and love point to this. Those who have experienced this often say that when they came back to life on earth they realised that life here is not the end, but just the preparation for the next life. And they said they would have preferred to stay in that blissful state, even more than to come back to be with their family or to take care of their unfinished business on earth. They had this experience not as some sort of fantasy, or a dream of an unreal and unrealisable world, but rather as something real, a foretaste of what awaits us if we live and die well. The fact that so many people, of different ages and religious beliefs, have had the same experience points to a reality, not a fantasy.

Heaven

Yes, heaven is for real. We have not only human experience to tell us that, but also the very word of God in Scripture. Jesus Christ himself promises it to those who live charity on earth. In his description of the judgment, he speaks of the Son of man coming to judge mankind and saying to those on his right hand: "Come, O blessed of my Father, inherit the kingdom prepared for you from the foundation of the world; for I was hungry and you gave me food, I was thirsty and you gave me drink, I was a stranger and you welcomed me ... And they will go away ... into eternal life" (*Matt* 25:34-46).

Christ also speaks of heaven to his apostles on the night before he died on the cross. In what we call the Last Supper, he told them: "In my Father's house are many rooms; if it were not so, would I have told you that I go to prepare a place for you? And when I go and prepare a place for you, I will come again and will take you to myself, that where I am you may be also" (*John* 14:2-3). This is a beautiful image of heaven: a room in the Father's house. When we die, we go home, home to the house of our heavenly Father. Pope St John Paul II was convinced of this reality. A few hours before he died on 2 April 2005, he said to those with him, "Let me go to the Father's house."

The joy of heaven is indescribable. St Paul, who felt himself caught up one day into heaven, could not describe the joy and beauty of what he experienced there. He could only write that he "heard things that cannot be told, which man may not utter (*2 Cor* 12:2-4). On another occasion he wrote: "What no eye has seen, nor ear heard, nor the heart of man conceived, what God has prepared for those who love him" (*1 Cor* 9:9).

St Paul also describes heaven as seeing God face to face: "For now we see in a mirror dimly, but then face to face. Now I know in part; then I shall understand fully, even as I have been fully understood" (*1 Cor* 13:12). As he says, here on earth we know God only in part, through the world he has made, and through what he has revealed to us in Jesus Christ and the Scriptures. But we don't see him. We can hardly imagine what it would be like to behold God's majesty, his infinite beauty, and to do so directly, face to face. In heaven we will do that.

If we wonder how we will be able to see God face to face when he is pure spirit, we can begin by remembering that when people in near-death experiences saw heaven, they sometimes recognised their loved ones there, even though those loved ones were there not in their body but only in their soul. It will be the same with seeing God. The understanding is that we will be given a special help, known as the Light of Glory, to see him. In any case, what is certain is that the most important aspect of our joy in heaven will be being with God in all his glory and knowing ourselves loved by him, with unimaginable love.

The last book of the Bible, the book of Revelation, describes the vast number and immense joy of those in heaven:

> After this I looked, and behold, a great multitude which no man could number, from every nation, from all tribes and peoples and tongues, standing before the throne and before the Lamb, clothed in white robes, with palm branches in their hands, and crying out with a loud voice, 'Salvation belongs to our God who sits upon the throne, and to the Lamb... They shall hunger no more, neither thirst any more; the sun shall not strike them, nor any scorching heat. For the Lamb in the midst of the throne will be their shepherd, and he will guide them to springs of living water; and God will wipe away every tear from their eyes (*Rev* 7:9-10, 16-17).

The Lamb of course, is Jesus Christ himself, who was called the Lamb of God. Compared with the joy that awaits us in heaven, any suffering we can undergo on earth is as nothing. St Paul, who experienced frequent and intense suffering on earth – scourging, being beaten with rods, being stoned, shipwreck, cold, heat, hunger, thirst – says: "I consider that the sufferings of this present time are not worth comparing with the glory that is to be revealed to us" (*Rom* 8:18).

The teaching of the Church, developed over the centuries, is expressed in the *Catechism of the Catholic Church*: "Those who die in God's grace and friendship and are perfectly purified live for ever with Christ. They are like God for ever, for they 'see him as he is,' face to face" (*CCC* 1023). The Catechism goes on to summarise all this, describing the joy of heaven: "This perfect life with the Most Holy Trinity – this communion of life and love with the Trinity, with the Virgin Mary, the angels and all the blessed – is called 'heaven'. Heaven is the ultimate end and fulfilment of the deepest human longings, the state of supreme, definitive happiness" (*CCC* 1024).

As this point says, the greatest source of joy in heaven will be sharing in the communion of life and love with God himself, who reveals himself as a trinity of persons: Father, Son and Holy Spirit, in one God. In addition, those in heaven will delight in the presence of Jesus' mother Mary, the angels, and the vast number of the blessed, all those who, over the centuries, have died and gone to heaven. Among them will be members of our own families and friends who have preceded us in death. It will be like an immense family reunion.

What is more, heaven is "the ultimate end and fulfilment of the deepest human longings". As we saw earlier, our human longings are never fully satisfied here on earth. We long for more than we can possibly attain here below. There is something in us, our spiritual soul, which is in some way unlimited, which cannot be satisfied with the limited goods we can find on earth. Only in heaven will we find the complete happiness we long for. Not for nothing did St Augustine write to God: "You made us for you, and our heart is restless until it rests in you" (*Confessions*, 1, 1, 1). Only in God, who is the infinite good, will our heart truly rest.

And heaven is the state of "supreme, definitive happiness". It is supreme, the highest possible. On earth we have much happiness, very much, but it is not the total happiness we seek. There is a reason for this. We find happiness when we find a good. The good might be a loving spouse, a new baby, a good meal, a good book, a good holiday... All of these are finite, limited goods which cannot completely satisfy the unlimited longing of our heart. As evidence of this, some of the richest people, who seem to have everything, are very unhappy. Only the infinite good, God himself, can truly satisfy us.

Our happiness in heaven is not only supreme; it is "definitive", everlasting, without ever lessening. Again, on earth our happiness comes and goes: the good film ends, we finish the book or the holiday, our new car wears out... But not the happiness of heaven. We will be in union with God and all the blessed forever. Our happiness will not end, nor will it lessen in any way. This is difficult to imagine, but we have God's word that this is how it will be. It is truly something to look forward to. The Catechism goes on to describe the beauty and joy of heaven:

> This mystery of blessed communion with God and all who are in Christ is beyond all understanding and description. Scripture speaks of it in images: life, light, peace, wedding feast, wine of the kingdom, the Father's house, the heavenly Jerusalem, paradise: 'no eye has seen, nor ear heard, nor the heart of man conceived, what God has prepared for those who love him' (*1 Cor 2:9*; *CCC* 1027).

The idea of eternal life in heaven may suggest to us that it may somehow be boring, always the same. This might be the case if eternity were an endless succession of time. But it is not. Pope Benedict XVI writes of it in his encyclical *Spe salvi*, Saved by hope (2007):

> It would be like plunging into the ocean of infinite love, a moment in which time – the before and after – no longer exists. We can only attempt to grasp the idea that such a moment is life in the full sense, a plunging ever anew into the vastness of being, in which we are simply overwhelmed with joy. This is how Jesus expresses it in Saint John's gospel: "I will see you again and your hearts will rejoice, and no one will take your joy from you" (1John 16:22; SS n. 12).

In view of the overwhelming joy that is heaven, it is worthwhile sacrificing everything that takes us away from God, and to endeavour to live a good life, so that one day we will be with God forever in heaven.

Who can go to heaven? Must one be a Christian, or a believer in some other religion, or at least a believer in God? The short answer is that, in principle, everyone can go to heaven. St Paul writes that God "desires all men to be saved and to come to the knowledge of the truth" (*1 Tim* 2:4). God created every human being in his image and likeness and his plan is that everyone should be with him in paradise. He excludes no one. Some may exclude themselves, as we will see when we study hell, but that is their own choosing, not God's.

The Catholic Church, in the Second Vatican Council, a gathering of the world's bishops held in Rome from 1962 to 1965, addressed this question. After considering the relationship of the Church to many different groups of people – other Christians, Jews, Muslims, those who do not know Christ – it finished with those who do not even know God. It declared: "Nor shall divine providence deny the assistance necessary for salvation to those who, without any fault of theirs, have not yet arrived at an explicit knowledge of God, and who, not without grace, strive to lead a good life. Whatever good or truth is found amongst them is considered by the Church to be a preparation for the gospel and given by him who enlightens all men that they may at length have life" (Dogmatic Constitution on the Church *Lumen Gentium*, n. 16).

As this point says, even those who do not know God can be saved and go to heaven. They must be in this position through no fault of their own and they must strive to lead a good life, which includes being sorry for their wrongdoing, or sins. What is more, God will give them, and everyone, all the grace, the help they need to go to heaven. Now it is up to them – to each one of us. Our eternal destiny is in our hands.

With eternal life with God in heaven as the goal of life, as the goal of everyone's life, we should not be sad if misfortune comes our way. It will come, in various forms. Even if the doctor tells us we have cancer and we are going to die, we should not be sad. We are drawing ever closer to the greatest happiness imaginable.

We can recall the story I told in *Dying to Live* about the Sydney surgeon going to visit a patient who was dying of cancer of the stomach and wasn't expected to live long. When the surgeon walked into the room, the patient put down his paper and greeted him with a big smile and said, "Doctor, I know it's not normally done, but I want you to be honest with me and please give me an indication of how long I have to live." The doctor, with some hesitation, told him possibly six to twelve weeks, but this could vary, depending on the circumstances.

The patient smiled broadly and thanked him, as if relieved by the news. The doctor was astounded. He had never seen such a reaction to what he considered the equivalent of a death sentence. He was more used to hearing something along the lines of, "If there is a God, please help me, and don't let me die." He asked the patient the reason for his joy-filled response, and the answer dumbfounded him: "Well Doctor, I know where I am going and now you have given me a timeline, so I can get my affairs in order and prepare to meet my Maker". What a great way to look on a death sentence! For this patient it was a blessing, information on how much time remained to prepare for the greatest joy of all, the leap into eternity with God.

Hell

While heaven is the destination we naturally long for, we should be aware that there is another destination for those who, by their own free choice, do not deserve to go there. Hell is a frightening prospect. It means eternal separation from the God for whom we were made and from his love, a love which can fill us with joy and peace more than we can possibly imagine. At the same time it means eternal punishment, likened to fire. That is indeed daunting, something no one would want to experience.

In a sense, it is only to be expected that there should be a hell. Why? Because there is a deep-seated sense in all of us that there should be justice, that good deeds should be rewarded and evil ones punished. And since this does not always happen here on earth, our sense of justice argues that, if there is life after death, at least there should be justice in the next life. That does not prove that there is a hell, but it does respond to our natural desire for justice, so that it would be good if there was one. For someone else, of course, not for ourselves.

To be sure, it was Jesus Christ himself who told us about hell. Many times. In his description of the judgment at the end of the world he speaks of the Son of man coming in his glory and gathering before him all the nations, separating them as the shepherd separates the sheep from the goats. After describing the reward of eternal life to be given to the righteous, he says to the others: "Depart from me, you cursed, into the eternal fire prepared for the devil and his angels; for I was hungry and you gave me no food, I was thirsty and you gave me no drink ... And they will go away into eternal punishment, but the righteous into eternal life" (*Matt* 25:31-46).

In this passage Christ mentions the two principal forms of punishment in hell. In saying "Depart from me" he is speaking of the eternal separation of the soul from God, known as the "pain of loss". And in "the eternal fire prepared for the devil and his angels" he is speaking of the "pain of sense", the pain of fire. Even though it is experienced only in the soul, the pain is exceedingly intense, likened to fire in many passages of the Bible. And, of course, the punishment of hell is eternal, forever. Just like the eternal state of bliss, which is heaven.

If the pain of fire sounds great, the pain of not being with God is greater. St John Chrysostom, who died in 407 AD, writes: "Unbearable is the fire of hell – who does not know it? – and dreadful are its torments; but, if one were to heap a thousand hell-fires one on the other, it would be as nothing compared with the punishment of being excluded from the blessed glory of heaven ... and of being compelled to hear Christ say: 'I know you not'" (*Homilies on Matthew*, 23, 9).

So it is Jesus himself, who loves us so much that he died on the cross for us and who wants all to be saved, who speaks of eternal punishment. Moreover, he makes it clear that it is easy to go to hell: "Enter by the narrow gate; for the gate is wide and the way is easy, that leads to destruction, and those who enter by it are many. For the gate is narrow and the way is hard, that leads to life, and those who find it are few" (*Matt* 7:13-14).

By these words Jesus seems to be saying that it is much easier to go to hell, to "destruction", than to heaven, to "life". If we think about it, we would probably agree. We all have a natural tendency to do the wrong thing: to be proud, self-centred, lazy, self-indulgent, deceitful, unkind, dishonest, greedy, etc. And we know well that unless we struggle to resist these tendencies, we can easily fall into a way of life that is seriously disordered, in which we do grave harm to ourselves and others. If we are not sorry for these offences and we do nothing to repair the harm we have caused, we could go to hell.

Jesus' teaching in the Bible, then, is clear. But does the Church still believe in hell? Of course it does. It has always believed in hell. According to the *Catechism of the Catholic Church*, "The teaching of the Church affirms the existence of hell and its eternity. Immediately after death the souls of those who die in a state of mortal sin descend into hell, where they suffer the punishments of hell, 'eternal fire'. The chief punishment of hell is eternal separation from God, in whom alone man can possess the life and happiness for which he was created and for which he longs" (*CCC* 1035). By "mortal sin", the Catechism means serious, grave sin, such as murder, adultery, theft of a large sum of money, etc. The word "mortal", by the way, comes from the Latin word for death. Mortal sin is death-dealing to the soul.

But, we might ask, how can a good God send anyone to eternal punishment? The answer is simple. He doesn't. God doesn't send anyone to hell. He wants all to be saved and to come to the knowledge of the truth (cf. *1 Tim* 2:4), and he gives everyone sufficient help, or grace, to be saved (cf. *2 Cor* 12:9). It is the person who sends himself, or herself, to hell. The Catechism puts it like this: "To die in mortal sin without repenting and accepting God's merciful love means remaining separated from him forever by our own free choice. This state of definitive self-exclusion from communion with God and the blessed is called 'hell'" (*CCC* 1033).

As this point implies, all someone needs to do to escape hell and go to heaven is to be sorry for their sins, especially the serious ones, the mortal sins. This is not difficult. When the person is truly sorry, he accepts the merciful love of God, who is always ready to forgive the sinner. If, however, he remains obstinate in his sins, without being sorry, he is in effect choosing hell.

But couldn't God take everyone to heaven? He could. But it would mean not respecting the freedom he gave us, and God is too much of a father to do that. The then Cardinal Joseph Ratzinger, later Pope Benedict XVI, explains: "God never, in any case, forces anyone to be saved. God accepts man's freedom. He is no magician, who will in the end wipe out everything that has happened and wheel out his happy ending. He is a true father; a creator who assents to freedom, even when it is used to reject him. That is why God's all-embracing desire to save people does not involve the actual salvation of all men. He allows us the power to refuse. God loves us; we need only to summon up the humility to allow ourselves to be loved" (*God is Near Us*, Ignatius 2003, pp. 36-37).

The British writer C.S. Lewis says something similar in his book *The Great Divorce* (1945), speaking about the end of life: "There are only two kinds of people in the end: those who say to God, 'Thy will be done', and those to whom God says, in the end, 'Thy will be done'. All that are in hell choose it. Without that self-choice there could be no hell. No soul that seriously and constantly desires joy will ever miss it. Those who seek find. To those who knock it is opened" (p. 58).

God could not have done more to keep us out of hell. He sent his eternal Son to become man in Jesus Christ, who suffered and died on a cross to open for us the way to heaven. Christ told us about the reality of hell so that we would be warned of what awaits us if we die without sorrow for our sins. He gives us all the help we need throughout our life to do what is right and avoid doing what is wrong. He is always ready to forgive us when we come to him with true sorrow for our sins. He could not do more. Now it is up to us.

What then can we do to avoid going to hell? First and foremost, struggle to do as much good as we can, growing in love for God and our neighbour. Second, try to commit fewer sins, especially the more serious ones. If we still fall, and we probably will, be truly sorry for our sins and resolve to lead a better life. And then, make every effort to change our ways, to give up the bad habits that led us into serious sin. Strive to be that better person that God wants us to be and that we too want to be.

Our goal in life

Knowing the destination of our journey through life, and how important it is to reach it, we do well to ask ourselves, in all sincerity: What in fact is my goal in life? What do I really hope to achieve? What do I regard as important? When I die, what would I like to leave behind? While we will all have our personal goals, we should remember that they should always be subordinated to the one, the only goal, that really matters: to go to heaven.

We can have all the money we want, but that in itself will not bring us the happiness we seek. That happiness can only come when we store up treasure in heaven through our good deeds. We can be highly regarded by others, but that will not guarantee us heaven either. The only one whose view of us really matters is God. He knows everything about us, and he will be our judge when we come before him at the end of our life.

All of this can help us reconsider our priorities in life. Perhaps some of our priorities up until now have not been the right ones. They were not leading us to be the good person we want to be, the good person who will go to heaven when we die. Anything that leads us astray, away from God, we must reject as worthless. Or even worse than worthless, because it actually takes us away from our destination.

The true measure of success in life is not money, or reputation, or awards received. After all, we can't take our money, our reputation or our awards with us when we die and come before God in the judgment. What we do take is our moral goodness, our faith in God, our love for others expressed in deeds. This is what assures us that we are on the way to heaven, to eternital life with God.

For this reason we shouldn't worry about what other people

think of us. Whether they think well of us or not doesn't make any difference when we come before God. We can be the biggest scoundrel in the opinion of some, or the greatest saint in the eyes of others, but it doesn't matter. The only one whose opinion of us matters is God. He will be our judge and he knows us. He knows us better than we know ourselves. He knows whether we are a scoundrel or a saint.

At the same time as we consider our personal goals and whether they are aligned with the only goal that matters, we can find it helpful to consider how we react to upsets, disappointments in life. They will come. Throughout our life, in addition to the joys and successes, there will be many failures. At least, failures from the human point of view. We didn't get that job or that promotion. The business we began with so much hope failed and we had to close it. That promising investment went sour and we lost a lot of money. We didn't marry the love of our life, and the marriage we entered into wasn't a happy one.

How do we respond to these upsets? Normally we suffer quite a bit and sometimes for a long time. We may even get depressed and become difficult to live with for those around us. A good way to face the upsets, no matter how serious they may be, is to put them in the context of our true goal in life and ask: Does this take me away from God, from my journey to heaven? Very often we will find that it doesn't. Yes, we lost a lot of money, but we haven't lost our faith in God and in the promise of heaven.

The failure may even be a blessing in that it brings us back to what really matters in life. Perhaps we were too absorbed in our work and business deals and were neglecting our family or our spiritual life. We lost focus, but it has woken us up and made us realise that we had our priorities in the wrong place. Fortunately, we still have time to realign our life on the one destination that is all important. After all, we desperately want to spend eternity with God. Yes, with God. Eternity is not just a state. It is eternal life with a person, with God. But who is this God?

4

THE GOD WHO AWAITS US

As we have seen, the goal of our journey of life is heaven, where we will see God face to face and be with him for all eternity. It is God who created the universe and who created each one of us through the love of our parents. He desperately wants all of us to be with him in heaven and he does all he can to get us there. Now it is up to us.

A big help in setting out on this journey and continuing until the end is getting to know this God, who loves us so much. It's a bit like going to visit our grandmother or some other significant person in our life. If we know that person well, and he or she means a lot to us, we are eager to see them. The more we know them and how much they have done for us, the more eager we are. If that is the case with going to see a human being, it is much more the case when the person we are going to see is God himself, who is everything for us. But many people do not really know God. They may know that he exists and that he created the universe, but they don't know him personally and, as a result, they don't love him.

A good starting point is to consider what the thousands of people who have had near-death experiences have discovered about God. Whether they believed in God or not beforehand, whether their idea of God was this or that, their common experience when their soul went to heaven was love. Overwhelming love. And with love, joy, overwhelming joy. They all experienced it and it changed their lives forever. When they came back, they invariably realised that they had their priorities wrong and that what really mattered was to love God and others more. And, of course, they didn't fear death anymore, but rather looked forward to experiencing the love of God in heaven, this time forever.

God is love

God is love. This tells us something that was already there in the Bible – that God is love. St John tells us so in his first letter: "God is love, and he who abides in love abides in God, and God abides in him" (*1 John* 4:16). This is an awesome truth. Not only does God love, but he is love. His very nature is love, infinite love.

And because he is love, he naturally wants to share, to communicate, his love. And so he created the universe, and he created us human beings in his image and likeness. And when we separated ourselves from him by sin, he sent his Son Jesus Christ to redeem us, to reconcile us with him by his death on the cross. "For God so loved the world that he gave his only-begotten Son, that whoever believes in him should not perish but have eternal life. For God sent the Son into the world, not to condemn the world, but that the world might be saved through him" (*John* 3:16-17).

Pope Benedict XVI, in his first encyclical letter to the whole world, titled *God is Love* (2005), wrote: "We have come to believe in God's love: in these words the Christian can express the fundamental decision of his life. Being Christian is not the result of an ethical choice or a lofty idea, but the encounter with an event, a person, which gives life a new horizon and a decisive direction" (n. 1). What Pope Benedict wrote about Christians applies to every human being. God loves everyone, no matter who they are or what their religious belief. And it is this love of God for everyone that "gives life a new horizon and a decisive direction". It is this love that sets us off on our journey of life to encounter God and his infinite love forever in heaven.

Where we see God's love in its fulness is in the death of his Son Jesus on the cross. Jesus freely chose to offer himself as a sacrifice in order to redeem us, to reconcile us with the Father. He said: "For this reason the Father loves me, because I lay down my life, that I may take it again. No one takes it from me, but I lay it down of my own accord" (*John* 10:17-18).

In the Last Supper Jesus told the apostles, "Greater love has no man than this, that a man lay down his life for his friends" (*John* 15:13). The following day, he laid down his life for all mankind. In a real sense, he went beyond what he had told the apostles. Jesus was not man laying down his life, he was God. And he was not laying down his life for his friends, but for a sinful humanity estranged from him by sin. Truly, there is no greater love than this. St John sums it up in his Gospel: "Having loved his own who were in the world, he loved them to the end" (*John* 13:1).

Christ was dying out of love, not only for the whole of humanity, but for every single person individually. He loves everyone, even you and me. Pope Francis, in his letter to the youth of the world *Christus vivit*, Christ is alive (2019), wrote: "The very first truth I would tell each of you is this: 'God loves you'. It makes no difference whether you have already heard it or not. I want to remind you of it. God loves you. Never doubt this, whatever may happen to you in life. At every moment, you are infinitely loved" (n. 112). This truth naturally moves us to want to meet God and experience his love in heaven.

It makes no difference what religion you may have, whether you believe in God or not, or whether you find yourself very far from God through your many sins. God loves you. And he wants you to be with him in heaven. Naturally, he wants you to change your life so that you can be worthy of going to heaven. And it's never too late.

One great sinner who lived far from God but then changed radically and became a great saint was St Augustine. In his *Confessions*, addressing himself to God, he laments his earlier life and slowness in coming to God, caught up, as he was, in love for the world:

> Late have I loved you, O Beauty so ancient and so new; late have I loved you! For behold you were within me, and I outside; and I sought you outside and in my ugliness fell upon those lovely things that you have made. You were with me and I was not with you. I was kept from you by those things, yet had they not been in you, they would not have been at all. You called and cried to me and broke open my deafness: and you sent forth your beams and shone upon me and chased away my blindness: you breathed fragrance upon me, and I drew in my breath and do now pant for you: I tasted you, and now hunger and thirst for you; you touched me, and I have burned for your peace (*Confessions*, Book 10, 26, 37).

So God loves everyone, and he will do all he can to bring everyone to be with him. When they find him, they, like St Augustine, will naturally relish the encounter, and they will hunger and thirst to be with God forever in heaven.

God is mercy

A big help in that quest is to know that the God who wants to take you with him to heaven is a God of mercy. By the way, this God is your God, no matter what religion you may have or have had in the past. There is only God and he is the God, indeed the Father, of all.

Sometimes people conceive of God as a God of anger, ever ready to punish, as if he made human beings so that he could make them suffer. But God is not like that. The Scriptures describe him as a God who is "ever rich in mercy". In the Old Testament book of Exodus, God describes himself as "a God merciful and gracious, slow to anger, and abounding in mercy and faithfulness, keeping merciful love for thousands, forgiving iniquity and transgression and sin" (*Exodus* 34:5-7). The prophet Isaiah describes God's mercy in graphic terms: "Can a woman forget her sucking child, that she should have no compassion on the son of her womb? Even these may forget, yet I will not forget you. Behold, I have carved you on the palms of my hands" (*Isaiah* 49:15-16).

Jesus Christ himself forgave many sinners, including a woman caught in the act of adultery. To make it easy for people to have their sins forgiven, he gave his Church a way for priests to forgive sins in his name: the sacrament of Penance, or Confession. And he related the beautiful parable, or story, of the prodigal son. It involves a young man who asked his father for the share of inheritance that was his, so he could go away and explore a different lifestyle. The father gave him the money and he left. But, as his father no doubt feared, he fell in with the wrong company, spent all his money and committed many sins. Now without any money, he was given a job feeding pigs, and he saw that the pigs had more to eat than he did. He then decided to go back to his father and tell him he was sorry for what he had done, asking to be taken back, not as a son, but as a hired servant. To his joy, when his father saw him coming he ran out, embraced and kissed him and prepared a fatted calf for a meal to celebrate his son's homecoming. This is an image of God, the merciful father, who will always take back a son or daughter of his who returns with sorrow for what they have done, no matter how many sins they have committed (cf. *Luke* 15:11-32).

And St Paul, in his letter to those in Ephesus, reminds us how, when we were sunk in our sins, God in his mercy raised us up:

> And you he made alive, when you were dead through the trespasses and sins in which you once walked, following the course of this world, following the prince of the power of the air, the spirit that is now at work in the sons of disobedience. Among these we all once lived in the passions of our flesh, following the desires of body and mind, and so we were by nature children of wrath, like the rest of mankind. But God, who is rich in mercy, out of the great love with which he loved us, even when we were dead through our trespasses, made us alive together with Christ (by grace you have been saved), and raised us up with him, and made us sit with him in the heavenly places in Christ Jesus, that in the coming ages he might show the immeasurable riches of his grace in kindness toward us in Christ Jesus (*Eph* 2:1-7).

Someone who spoke powerfully about the mercy of God was Sister Josefa Menendez, a Spanish nun who was born in Madrid in 1890. As I wrote in *Dying to Live*, Sister Josefa was allowed to experience the suffering of souls in hell. She related her revelations in her book *The Way of Divine Love*. There she spoke of Jesus' ardent desire to save souls from going to hell and his mercy in forgiving repentant sinners. Jesus says: "I would like [those living with sin] to understand that it is not the fact of being in sin that ought to keep them from me. They must never think that there is no remedy for them, nor that they have forfeited forever the love that once was theirs ... No, poor souls, the God who has shed all his Blood for you has no such feelings for you." As Jesus says, it is not the fact of sin that keeps people from God, but their lack of sorrow. God is merciful and he will always forgive us. All we need to do is ask him for forgiveness.

God is Father

God is not some far-off, almighty creator of the universe, who doesn't care about individual human beings. He reveals himself as Father and he regards all of us as his children. All of us. All eight billion of us. This is an immensely consoling thought. It is Jesus Christ who reminds us constantly of this reality.

With regard to prayer, Jesus says in his well-known Sermon on the Mount: "But when you pray, go into your room and shut the door and pray to your Father who is in secret; and your Father who sees in secret will reward you" (*Matt* 6:6). Yes, God our Father knows each one of us and will reward us for our good deeds. Moreover, "And in praying do not heap up empty phrases as the Gentiles do; for they think that they will be heard for their many words. Do not be like them, for your Father knows what you need before you ask him" (*Matt* 6:7-8). We don't need to use eloquent phrases to talk with God. We are his children, and we can talk with him however we want. What is more, like the good Father he is, he already knows what we need before we ask him.

Jesus then goes on to give us what has come to be known as the Lord's Prayer: "Pray then like this: "Our Father who art in heaven, hallowed be thy name. Thy kingdom come. Thy will be done on earth as it is in heaven. Give us this day our daily bread; and forgive us our trespasses as we forgive those who trespass against us; and lead us not into temptation, but deliver us from evil" (*Matt* 6:9-13). In this simple prayer we praise God, ask him for all our needs, and beg him to forgive our sins.

We all have cares and even worries. Most often they are real, legitimate. We have lost our job, our spouse has been diagnosed with cancer, we can't meet our mortgage repayments, we don't know how we are going to solve some problem. Okay, but we have been through similar situations in the past and, somehow, we got through those. Surely, we will get through our problems now. In these stressful situations we tend to forget that there is another powerful factor at work besides our human efforts. It is God. God all powerful, all merciful, all loving. And he is our Father.

To put us at ease and to remind us of the power of God in these situations, St Peter writes: "Humble yourselves therefore under the mighty hand of God, that in due time he may exalt you. Cast all your anxieties on him, for he cares about you" (*1 Pet* 5:6-7).

Jesus, too, tells us not to worry, because our Father God is looking after us. "Therefore do not be anxious, saying 'What shall we eat?' or 'What shall we drink?' or 'What shall we wear?' For the Gentiles seek all these things; and your heavenly Father knows that you need them all. But seek first his kingdom and his righteousness, and all these things shall be yours as well" (*Matt* 6:31-33).

Elsewhere Jesus says: "Ask, and it will be given you; seek, and you will find; knock, and it will be opened to you. For every one who asks receives, and he who seeks finds, and to him who knocks it will be opened. Or what man of you, if his son asks him for bread, will give him a stone? Or if he asks for a fish, will give him a serpent? If you then, who are evil, know how to give good gifts to your children, how much more will your Father who is in heaven give good things to those who ask him!" (*Matt* 7:7-11) Yes, God is our Father and he will always give us good things.

This does not mean, of course, that he will always give us what we are asking of him, or that he will give it immediately. Earthly fathers don't always give their children everything they ask for either. Sometimes fathers, and mothers, know that it would not be in the best interests of their children to give them what they are asking for. When the parents say no, the children are disappointed and even angry at times, but the parents hold their ground. They love their children and they want what is best for them.

God our Father is like that, except that, being divine, he knows even better what is truly good for his children. Our reaction in these cases must be to pray with faith to God to help us through the difficult situation, to know that he always hears and answers us, and to accept whatever he gives us. It will always be for the best, even if we don't see it that way. Often, later in life, we look back at the situation and we realise that it was truly for the best.

One of the mysteries of God's fatherly love is the reality of suffering. God loves us and yet he allows us to suffer. He doesn't always give us what we want and sometimes what he gives us is something that makes us suffer. Could a good father do that? Of course. Earthly fathers do it too, when they discipline their children moved by love.

We read in the *Letter to the Hebrews*: "For the Lord disciplines him whom he loves, and chastises every son whom he receives... God is treating you as sons; for what son is there whom his father does not discipline?" (*Heb* 12:6-7) Just as earthly fathers discipline their children, making them suffer in some way in order to correct them and teach them virtue, so God treats his children in the same way. Moreover, as the Letter goes on to say, our earthly fathers "disciplined us for a short time at their pleasure, but he disciplines us for our good, that we may share his holiness" (*Heb* 12:10). Whatever allows us to share in God's holiness must surely be a blessing, even if it seems painful at the time.

If we want evidence that God the Father disciplines even his own beloved children, we need only look at Jesus Christ, whom the Father calls "my beloved Son in whom I am well pleased" (*Matt* 17:5). Christ, the eternal Son of the Father, suffered more than we ever will and he was the most beloved of his Father God. God says he will discipline those whom he loves in the last book of the Bible, Revelation: "Those whom I love, I reprove and chasten; so be zealous and repent" (*Rev* 3:19).

So, as we go along our journey to heaven, loving and trusting in God our Father, we should not complain or be angry if we experience suffering. God is treating us as his children.

God is provident

The action of God in always providing for us and giving us what is best is what we call divine providence. The word providence comes from the Latin word providere and it means essentially to foresee, or to provide. God foresees everything. He is outside of time and he sees everything, past, present and future, at once. And he knows everything. After all, he made everything. And, as he is love, he loves everything and everyone. In his providence he watches over everything and everyone and guides it gently to its end.

His providence reaches every single person and every aspect of our life. Sometimes we may wonder what is going on in our life, why life is as it is, or why the world is in such a dreadful state. But the knowledge that God is our Father and that his providence reaches everywhere, can fill us with trust and confidence. We may not know what is happening or why it is happening, or what the future holds, but God our Father does. We need not worry.

He is the Lord of history. He has the whole world in his hands. Nothing happens but what he permits or wills to happen. If right now the world is in a mess, or we have personal problems, God knows that and he will bring good out of it. He always does, even if we don't see it at the time.

Consider, for example, natural disasters – floods, wild fires, earthquakes, tsunamis, volcanic eruptions – with all the loss of life and devastation they bring. They wreak tremendous havoc. They are simply consequences of the nature of the planet on which we live. But at the same time, through them, thousands of people are led to give of themselves, of their time and effort, or of their money or possessions to help the afflicted, to alleviate in some way their suffering. This manifestation of solidarity with people they don't even know is a great good for all concerned.

In any case, as we have seen, a good question to ask ourselves when we are troubled by something is whether this takes us away from God, from our final destination of heaven. Only what does that is a true tragedy. If it doesn't, in the greater scheme of things, it is not so bad after all. For example, we might have been diagnosed with terminal cancer. For people without faith, this can be devastating. Why me? Why now? I am still young and I have my whole life in front of me.

But when we consider the illness in the light of our journey to heaven, we see that, while it may involve pain and suffering, it doesn't take us away from God or heaven at all. It may even speed us along on that journey. If the goal of life is eternity with God in a state of indescribable happiness, then dying and going to heaven sooner can only be a good thing.

Let me tell you a story which I related in my book *The Final Exam – Preparing for the Judgment*. It involves a woman I knew, a Canberra mother of six school-age children who was dying of cancer in 1987. One day she wrote in her diary, addressing herself to Christ: "The pain in my chest is crushing me. As the pain crushed You as You struggled to breathe while you hung on the Cross. You are in my pain. I am in Yours. We are one – my God and I! What else can I ever ask for? In this You have given me proof of your love." This woman was greatly consoled by seeing herself united with Christ on the cross in the midst of her great pain. And she knew that soon she would be with him forever in heaven. Without that awareness, her pain might have seemed meaningless, even cruel. But in the providence of God, it was a blessing for her.

Or the case of another woman I knew well, who was dying of cancer and was in constant pain for months. One day her husband asked her why God was allowing her to suffer so much. She answered simply that her pain was part of God's plan to purify her of her sins, and that it was also purifying her husband, who was suffering with her.

This is the providence of God. It reaches to the whole universe and to every single being, especially to human beings, whom he made in his image and likeness. The *Catechism of the Catholic Church* teaches: "The witness of Scripture is unanimous that the solicitude of divine providence is concrete and immediate; God cares for all, from the least things to the great events of the world and its history. The sacred books powerfully affirm God's absolute sovereignty over the course of events: 'Our God is in the heavens; he does whatever he pleases' (*Psalm* 115:3). And so it is with Christ, 'who opens and no one shall shut, who shuts and no one opens' (*Rev* 3:7). As the book of Proverbs states: 'Many are the plans in the mind of a man, but it is the purpose of the Lord that will be established' (*Prov* 19:21; *CCC* 303).

We will meet Jesus too

In talking about meeting God in heaven, we should never forget that we will meet Jesus Christ there too. Jesus is the Son of God, as he so often said, and so we cannot separate him from the Father. At the same time, he is man, a man like us. A good number of the those who have had near-death experiences have described meeting Jesus in heaven.

The Father, Son and Holy Spirit, by the way, are three divine persons in what Christians call the Blessed Trinity. They are three persons in one God. This is a great mystery, which we cannot fully comprehend, but it has been clearly revealed in the Scriptures that make up the Bible.

And, if God is the Father of all, no matter what their religion, Jesus is the saviour of all too. As we have seen, "For God so loved the world that he gave his only-begotten Son, that whoever believes in him should not perish but have eternal life. For God sent the Son into the world, not to condemn the world, but that the world might be saved through him" (*John* 3:16-17). When we say "the world", we mean everyone. As we have seen, he "desires all men to be saved and to come to the knowledge of the truth" (*1 Tim* 2:4).

Jesus told his apostles in the Last Supper that he was going to heaven to prepare a place for them: "In my Father's house are many rooms; if it were not so, would I have told you that I go to prepare a place for you? And when I go and prepare a place for you, I will come again and will take you to myself, that where I am you may be also" (*John* 14:2-3). Yes, Jesus is in heaven, in the Father's house, and he wants all of us to be with him there.

Jesus is God, God almighty who created the universe along with the Father and the Holy Spirit. St John tells us: "He was in the world, and the world was made through him, yet the world knew him not" (*John* 1:10). Yet, at the same time that he is God almighty, Jesus has called us his friends: "No longer do I call you servants, for the servant does not know what his master is doing; but I have called you friends, for all that I have heard from my Father I have made known to you" (*John* 15:15). Again, because Jesus wants us all to be his friends, he naturally desires to have us with him in the Father's house in heaven.

He is there now, praying for us and earnestly desiring to welcome us into his Father's house, when God calls us to eternal life. When that time comes, we can be sure that he will give us a big embrace to welcome us home.

5

TALKING WITH GOD IN PRAYER

When we come to know God as our loving, provident Father, who watches over us in life and wants us to be with him forever in heaven, we are naturally inclined to want to spend time talking with him and listening to him. This is prayer. It is like talking with our parents, who love us and look after us in so many ways. Not to talk with them often during the day would be to offend them, and it would fail to satisfy a deep-seated need and desire of ours to talk with those we love and to listen to their advice. To love and to be loved.

What is more, if we are going to spend eternity with God, we want to get to know him more and spend time with him now on earth. The more we do this, the more we will grow in love for God and the more we will be desirous and deserving of spending eternity with him in heaven. Prayer can take many forms.

Vocal prayers

The most common and, in a sense, easy form of prayer is to say the various prayers we have learned and have come to love. This is what we call vocal prayer. Mind you, the word vocal can be misleading here. Vocal usually refers to the voice and so the word can suggest that vocal prayers are said out loud. That can be the case, especially when we pray together with others, but when we pray on our own, we usually pray silently. In any case, the most commonly understood meaning of vocal prayer is prayers with a fixed formula, which we recite.

When we use the word recite, we are alerted to a danger common to everyone: to recite the words without thinking of their meaning. Then we would be guilty of what Jesus Christ laments when he says, quoting the prophet Isaiah, "This people honours me with their lips, but their heart is far from me" (*Matt* 15:8; *Is* 29:13). Always, when we pray we are talking with God and we want to think of what we are saying and make the words our own.

There are many vocal prayers, and each religion has its own. What matters is to say some of these prayers, because they engage us with God, and there is only one God.

The psalms

For Jews and Christians, a favourite group of prayers is the psalms. There are 150 of them and they are believed to have been composed by King David, some 1000 years before Christ. The psalms were prayed by the people of God of the Old Testament, whether gathered together in the great feasts in Jerusalem, in the synagogues throughout the land, or in family homes. Some are historical, recalling the great events of salvation history, others express petition in times of need, or thanksgiving, lament, trust in God's providence, and always praise of God for his mighty deeds. Indeed, the word "psalm" means praise.

For Christians, the psalms look forward to the Messiah, Jesus Christ, and many of them refer to specific aspects and events of his life. When Jesus appeared to the apostles in the Upper Room on the evening of his resurrection, he told them that the psalms and other scriptures foretold that he would be put to death and rise again (cf. *Luke* 24:44-47). The Catholic Church uses the psalms in every celebration of its most important rite, the Mass. And the Divine Office, or Liturgy of the Hours, said each day by clergy and religious, is based on the psalms.

St Ambrose, a fourth-century Father of the Church, sums up the beauty of the psalms:

> What is more pleasing than a psalm? David expresses it well: "Praise the Lord, for a psalm is good: let there be praise of our God with gladness and grace!" Yes, a psalm is a blessing on the lips of the people, praise of God, the assembly's homage, a general acclamation, a word that speaks for all, the voice of the Church, a confession of faith in song (*In psalmum 1 enarratio*, 1, 9).

The Lord's Prayer

For Christians, the quintessential prayer is the Lord's Prayer, the Our Father. It was Jesus Christ himself who, in his Sermon on the Mount, taught the apostles to say it (cf. *Matt* 6:9-13). After praising the name of God, asking for his kingdom to come and his will to be done, it begs God for our daily bread, forgiveness of our sins, not to be led into temptation, and to be saved from the evil one. It is a complete prayer. A third-century writer, Tertullian, called the Our Father "truly the summary of the whole gospel" (*De orat.* 1). St Augustine adds: "Run through all the words of the holy prayers [in Scripture], and I do not think that you will find anything in them that is not contained and included in the Lord's Prayer" (*Ep.* 130, 12, 22). And St Thomas Aquinas sums it up:

> The Lord's Prayer is the most perfect of prayers ... In it we ask, not only for all the things we can rightly desire, but also in the sequence that they should be desired.

> This prayer not only teaches us to ask for things, but also in what order we should desire them (*STh* II-II, 83, 9).

Christians of all denominations say the Our Father, so the prayer is used by a great part of the family of mankind. For Catholics, the Our Father is used in every Mass and it is therefore well known. It is also commonly used in religious ceremonies and family prayers by other Christians.

The Hail Mary

A very popular prayer for Catholics is the Hail Mary. The first part of the prayer comes from the Scriptures. The words "Hail, full of grace, the Lord is with thee" were said by the Angel Gabriel to Jesus' mother Mary in announcing that she was to bear a son (cf. *Luke* 1:28). The next words, "Blessed art thou among women and blessed is the fruit of thy womb" were pronounced by Mary's kinswoman Elizabeth when Mary went to visit her (cf. *Luke* 1:42). Later were added the name "Jesus" and the conclusion, "Holy Mary, Mother of God, pray for us sinners now and at the hour of our death".

For all those who regard Mary as their mother, the Hail Mary is a much-loved prayer. It is a favourite with families and other groups, and of course with individuals.

The rosary

A favourite prayer for Catholics and some other Christians is the rosary, which grew out of popular piety. In the early centuries lay people had the custom of praying 150 Our Fathers, to accompany the monks in the monasteries, who were praying the 150 psalms in the Divine Office. Around the year 1000 the Our Father gave way to the Hail Mary. And gradually the 150 Hail Marys came to be divided into three sets of 50, forming the Joyful Mysteries, which consider various aspects of the infancy of Jesus; the Sorrowful Mysteries, which consider his passion and death; and the Glorious Mysteries, which consider his resurrection from the dead and his glorification in heaven, along with his mother Mary. In 2002 Pope John Paul II added the Luminous Mysteries, which consider various aspects of Christ's three years of public life and preaching.

The rosary is a very rich prayer, and this in several senses. It is, in the first place, a Trinitarian prayer. The rosary begins, as does every prayer, with the Sign of the Cross, invoking the three divine persons: "In the name of the Father, and of the Son, and of the Holy Cross." It includes the Apostles' Creed, which mentions each of the divine persons: "I believe in God the Father the Almighty... and in Jesus Christ his only-begotten Son... I believe in the Holy Spirit..." And after each mystery comes the Trinitarian prayer, "Glory be to the Father and to the Son and to the Holy Spirit..."

The rosary is also very much a *Christ-centred prayer*, and Christ is the centre of Christians' faith. As we have said, the mysteries of the rosary are the mysteries of the life of Christ. Who is there who, loving Christ, does not want to meditate on the principal moments of his life, a meditation which will help greatly to come to know, love and imitate him? We should not forget that Christ is in the centre, too, of every Hail Mary, in the words "blessed is the fruit of thy womb, Jesus".

But the rosary is best known and loved as a *Marian prayer*. The Hail Mary, in addition to being an act of praise of Christ, is also a praise of Mary in the words of the Archangel Gabriel and Mary's kinswoman Elizabeth: "Hail Mary, full of grace, the Lord is with thee; blessed art thou among women." Anyone who loves Jesus is happy to repeat fifty times that magnificent praise of his mother. And Mary is our mother too. St John relates how just before he died on the cross, Jesus entrusted his mother to St John, and the tradition has always seen in St John, all of us (cf. *Jn* 19:26-27). After all, the fourth of the Ten Commandments entreats us to "Honour thy father and thy mother."

The rosary is a rich prayer too in that it includes all the principal types of prayer. It is on the one hand a *vocal prayer*, made up of prayers with a fixed set of words, but it is also *mental prayer* or *meditation*, in that on reciting the decades one meditates on the mysteries they call to mind. Anyone who has meditated on the mysteries can attest to the numerous personal insights, affections or resolutions they have received from it over the years. Moreover, when the mind rests in loving contemplation of the mysteries, the rosary becomes also contemplative prayer, moving Pope St John Paul II to write: "The rosary belongs among the finest and most praiseworthy traditions of Christian contemplation" (Apost. Letter *Rosarium Virginis Mariae*, n. 5).

Another reason why the rosary is so popular must surely be that people find that their prayers to God through the rosary are often answered in remarkable ways. It is a very powerful prayer. The victory of the Christian navy over the Turks at the battle of Lepanto in the Mediterranean in 1571 is one example. With 208 galleys as against the 286 of the Turks, the Christian fleet under Don Juan of Austria routed the Turkish navy. On the day before the battle, Pope Pius V, without any human knowledge that the battle would be fought, had asked the religious men and women in the convents of Rome to pray the rosary for a successful outcome.

On a personal level, the number of people cured of illnesses, of marriages saved, of lives completely turned around through the recitation of the rosary is known only to the protagonists and to God. Even when one's prayers are not always answered in obvious ways, the regular recitation of the rosary has already shown its power in the increase in holiness of those who pray it. The exercise of such virtues as faith, hope, love, humility and perseverance in saying the rosary must surely sanctify those who pray it assiduously, as must meditation on the mysteries of the life of Jesus Christ and his mother Mary.

Not for nothing have so many Popes and saints recommended the rosary. One of the more recent examples was Pope St John Paul II, who was well known for his great devotion to the rosary. In an address on 29 October 1978, only two weeks after his election as Pope, he said: "The rosary is my favourite prayer. A marvellous prayer. Marvellous in its simplicity and its depth."

And in October 1981, on resuming his public life after the attempt on his life in May of that year, he said: "In the last few weeks I have had numerous proofs of kindness on the part of people all over the world. I want to express my gratitude in decades of the rosary, in order to be able to express it in prayer, as well as in a human way; in the prayer, so simple and so rich, that the rosary is. I cordially exhort everyone to recite it."

Meditation

If vocal prayers are prayers with fixed words, like the ones we have just considered, meditation, or mental prayer, is talking with God in our own words. St Teresa of Avila describes it up like this:

> Mental prayer is nothing else than an intimate friendship, a frequent heart-to-heart conversation with him by whom we know ourselves to be loved (*Life*, VIII).

Mental prayer is the most personal form of prayer, for we talk with God about whatever is in our heart at the time. It might be to thank him for a favour, ask him how to solve a particular problem, tell him we have had enough crosses and can't take any more, tell him we love him ... When we talk to God like this, we are using, in a sense, the book of life, the book of our day-to-day existence. St Josemaria Escriva, the founder of Opus Dei, speaks of this in his book *The Way*: "You write: 'To pray is to talk with God. But about what? About him, about yourself: joys, sorrows, successes and failures, noble ambitions, daily worries, weaknesses! And acts of thanksgiving and petitions: and Love and reparation. In a word, to get to know him and to get to know yourself: 'to get acquainted!'" (n. 91).

Apart from the book of life, another source of meditation can be a book like the Bible or a spiritual book, using it to pray about what one has just read. This makes meditation easier, because the topic is given in what we are reading, and we can draw many truths and ideas from it. We can then apply these ideas to our personal life and see how we can improve in some aspect.

Meditation is perhaps a more difficult form of prayer than saying vocal prayers, but it is usually more helpful, because we are praying about our personal situation at the time and asking God for lights.

Difficulties in prayer

Praying is not always easy. In fact, sometimes it can be downright difficult. That is understandable. The *Catechism of the Catholic Church* deals with this topic in a section titled, very appropriately and perhaps surprisingly, "The battle of prayer". It begins:

Prayer is both a gift of grace and a determined response on our part. It always presupposes effort. The great figures of prayer of the Old Covenant before Christ, as well as the Mother of God, the saints, and he himself, all teach us this: prayer is a battle. Against whom? Against ourselves and against the wiles of the tempter who does all he can to turn man away from prayer, away from union with God. We pray as we live, because we live as we pray. If we do not want to act habitually according to the Spirit of Christ, neither can we pray habitually in his name. The "spiritual battle" of the Christian's new life is inseparable from the battle of prayer (*CCC*, n. 2725).

The most obvious difficulty in prayer is simply that we cannot see God. It is easy to talk with someone we can see, like our parents or a friend, but more difficult when we cannot see them. One way to solve this problem is to imagine God, or Jesus Christ, or the Blessed Virgin Mary or some saint, sitting in front of us, looking at us when we pray. We can imagine their clothing, their eyes, their facial expression, and so on. In doing this, we are putting ourselves into the scene along with the person to whom we are praying, and this can make it easier to pray.

Another difficulty is finding the time to pray. We all have many things to do each day, and they impose themselves on us. We must do them – today! Where then does God fit into this picture? It is easy to convince ourselves that we simply don't have time to pray, at least not today. Maybe tomorrow. Maybe not then either. When we start to think this way, we should take a step back and look at our priorities, at what we regard as important in life. The question is easy: "How important is God in my life?" Going back to what we said at the beginning of this book, we are very good at organising ourselves in our day-to-day activities, but we can overlook organising ourselves for the most important activity of all: the journey to heaven.

Yes, there may be days when we are simply overwhelmed with activities, one after the other, and we convince ourselves that we really don't have time to pray. That may be the case. But even then, perhaps getting up a little earlier in the morning, we could set aside a little time to talk with God and ask his grace to do his will and to get through all the activities of the day with serenity and charity. In any case, the journey to heaven is the most important priority and we simply need to include it in our daily plan.

Back in the fourth century, St Jerome addressed this problem, writing to the mother of a family:

> Look after your house in such a way that you also give some rest to your soul. Choose an opportune place, somewhat away from the commotion of the family, and take yourself there as to a port, as one escaping from a great storm of worries. Calm, with the tranquillity of this retreat, the waves of thoughts which have been aroused by external matters. Put so much effort and fervour into the reading of the Sacred Scriptures, let your prayers be so frequent, let the thought of the next life be so firm and dense, that you easily make up in this time of rest for all the concerns of the remaining time. I am not telling you this as if trying to take you away from your family. Rather I would like you to learn and meditate there on how you should act towards your family (*Epist.* 148, 24).

But even when we include some prayer in our daily schedule, we should be careful not to let that time be too short. It is easy to convince ourselves that five or ten minutes is enough. How much we pray will depend, of course, on our personal circumstances. But the tendency will always be to pray too little rather than too much.

We must be careful too not to let our prayer depend on how we feel about praying on a given day. "I just don't feel like praying today" can be an easy excuse not to pray. This is a dangerous attitude. It subjects God and our relationship with him to feelings, and feelings come and go, as we all know. We don't apply that attitude to other aspects of life. We don't say, "I just don't feel like getting out of bed today, or going to work, or making the meals". There are some duties we must simply fulfil, no matter how we feel about them on a given day. Our duty to God, the most important person in our life, must surely have a top priority. In short, we must be people of will, not of whim.

A good way to avoid letting our feelings dominate us is to have regular times set aside for prayer each day, and to hold ourselves to these times no matter how we feel. For example, we might pray on rising in the morning, before going to bed at night, in prayer before meals, prayers with the family, a regular time for meditation…

Another difficulty we all face is distractions. We set out to talk with God and very quickly our mind has jumped to what we are going to do on the weekend, or what we need to buy when we go to the shop. This is normal. It is universal, and it should not be a reason for discouragement. St Thomas More, the Lord Chancellor of England and martyr under King Henry VIII, speaks about distractions in a humorous way:

> I wish that sometime we would make a special effort, right after finishing our prayers, to run over in our

minds the whole sequence of time we spent praying. What follies will we see there? How much absurdity and sometimes even foulness will we catch sight of? Indeed, we will be amazed that it was at all possible for our minds to dissipate themselves in such a short time among so many places at such great distance from each other, among so many different affairs, such various, such manifold, such idle pursuits. For if someone, just as an experiment should make a determined effort to make his mind touch upon as many and as diverse objects as possible, I hardly think that in such a short time he could run through such disparate and numerous topics as the mind, left to its own devices, ranges through while the mouth negligently mumbles through the hours of the Office and other much-used prayers (*The Sadness of Christ*, Scepter 1994, p. 18).

Yes, distractions are common. But that doesn't mean we should do nothing about them. What can we do? The first thing, as soon as we find our mind far from our intended topic, is to tell God we are sorry, that here we go again. And to ask his grace, his help, to return to the topic. We can tell him that we will consider the distraction after our prayer, if indeed it is important. Occasionally, the distraction might be about a topic that we would do well to bring into our prayer, especially if we are doing meditation, For example, the argument we had with our spouse last night, our discouragement with something that has happened at work, a concern about one of our children. These would be good topics to take to our prayer.

Yet another difficulty is what is known as spiritual dryness, or aridity. In this state we find ourselves habitually distant from God, dry, with no consolations, as if God weren't listening to us or he were distant. Many saints have experienced this, even for long periods of time. One of them was the great sixteenth-century mystic and reformer of the Carmelites, St Teresa of Avila. Many people think she was in constant ecstasy, totally caught up in God, when she prayed. Yet, in her account of her life she writes:

> It would have been impossible, I think, for me to persevere during the eighteen years for which I had to bear this trial and these great aridities due to my being unable to meditate. During all these years, except after receiving Communion, I never dared to begin to pray without a book. My soul was as much afraid to engage in prayer without one as if it were having to go and fight a host of enemies. With this help, which was a companionship to me and a shield with which I could parry the blows of my many thoughts, I felt comforted (*Life*, 4).

One of the most well-known saints in recent times who experienced great spiritual dryness, a real "dark night of the soul", was Mother Teresa of Calcutta, foundress of the Missionaries of Charity. For the last fifty years of her life she felt God distant, absent, even when she was praying. She related this in some of her letters and to her spiritual director. For example: "Where is my faith? Even deep down [...] there is nothing but emptiness and darkness. [...] When I try to raise my thoughts to Heaven, there is such convicting emptiness that those very thoughts return like sharp knives and hurt my very soul." But Mother Teresa persevered in prayer in spite of her dryness, and that was what made her the great saint that she was. What matters during times of spiritual dryness is to persevere in prayer, even when it seems cold and useless. Anyone will pray when they find consolation in it. Only a saint will pray when they find it hard.

So, the difficulties in prayer can take many forms. If we are tempted to give up prayer because of them, we should remember that the devil will be very happy with one more success if he succeeds in taking us away from prayer, from conversation with God.

Finding our own way

In the matter of prayer, each person is different. A prayer that is popular with one person may not be with another. And a Christian will pray in a different way from a person of another faith tradition. That isn't important. What matters is that, given that we are all on a journey to the same destination, to eternal life with the one God in heaven, we should get to know him and love him here on earth, using whatever forms of prayer we find helpful. After all, God is real, and heaven is real. The more we spend time with God through prayer and grow in love for him, the more desirous we will be to spend eternity with him in heaven and, as a result, the better we will live our life here on earth in order to deserve that eternal reward. For this reason, we should have regular times set aside to spend with God each day. It will help us keep God, and our reason for being on earth, in mind.

So prayer is important. It is essential. It is our personal relationship with the God who is waiting for us in heaven. The more we know and love him, the more eager we will be to spend eternity with him in heaven.

But, at the same time, we naturally get caught up in the affairs of this world, and this can take our mind and heart away from God. How we deal with this is our next topic.

6

Heart in God, not in goods

Living a busy life in a busy world can sometimes make it easy to forget why we are here in the first place: to enjoy eternity with God in heaven. We all experience this. What is more, we can tend naturally to fall in love with the world and its trappings. After all, our consumerist, materialistic society draws our mind to things, to the accumulation of more and more things, including things we don't really need. Then our goal becomes living "the good life" here below, keeping up with the neighbours. But forgetting what really matters. Even if we are battling, struggling to pay the bills month after month, this can happen. We worry about our finances and the bills piling up, and forget that there is something more important than this.

Getting our priorities right

We should remember what is in fact the first commandment, as expressed by Jesus Christ himself: "You shall love the Lord your God with all your heart, and with all your soul, and with all your mind. This is the great and first commandment" (*Matt* 22:37-38). Our first love is not the world and all its trappings. It is God himself, who created the world and who watches over it in his loving providence. The more we love God, the less anxious we will be about the cares of the world. After all, as we have seen, we will spend only a short time in this world, even though it be a hundred years, and then we will leave it to spend eternity in the next life. It is clear which is the more important.

Two thousand years ago Jesus Christ warned about it in his well-known Sermon on the Mount: "Therefore, I tell you, do not be anxious about your life, what you shall eat or what you shall drink, nor about your body, what you shall put on. Is not life more than food, and the body more than clothing? Look at the birds of the air: they neither sow nor reap nor gather into barns, and yet your heavenly Father feeds them." And he summed it up: "For the Gentiles seek all these things; and your heavenly Father knows that you need them all. But seek first his kingdom and his righteousness, and all these things shall be yours as well" (*Matt* 6:25-26, 32-33). As Jesus says, what comes first is not satisfying our material needs, but seeking the kingdom of God and his holiness. Then God will provide for our material needs as well.

Getting the balance right between managing our worldly affairs and keeping our eye on the goal has always been a challenge. In that same Sermon, Jesus said: "Do not lay up for yourselves treasures on earth, where moth and rust consume and where thieves break in and steal, but lay up for yourselves treasures in heaven, where neither moth nor rust consumes and where thieves do not break in and steal. For where your treasure is, there will you heart be also" (*Matt* 6:19-21). The last words give us food for thought and examination. We do well to ask ourselves from time to time: Where is my heart? Is it in goods, or in God? As Jesus says, where our treasure is, there is our heart. We want to be storing up treasure in heaven through our good deeds, our service to those around us, our life of prayer. Then we will be rich indeed. And when God calls us, we will be able to enjoy his company forever in heaven.

Lest we think we can store up treasure both on earth and in

heaven, loving both, Jesus warns us: "No one can serve two masters; for either he will hate the one and love the other, or he will be devoted to the one and despise the other. You cannot serve God and mammon" (*Matt* 6:24). That is, while we can have both God and goods in our life, we cannot serve both. As evidence of this, there have always been many wealthy people who were generous in giving of their wealth to the poor and to charitable causes. They did not serve their wealth; they were not attached to it.

St Paul, too, gives us some salutary advice in this regard:

> There is great gain in godliness with contentment; for we brought nothing into the world, and we cannot take anything out of the world; but if we have food and clothing, with these we shall be content. But those who desire to be rich fall into temptation, into a snare, into many senseless and hurtful desires that plunge men into ruin and destruction. For the love of money is the root of all evils; it is through this craving that some have wandered away from the faith and pierced their hearts with many pangs (*1 Tim* 6:6-10).

It is not money itself, but the love of money which is the root of all evils. Again, we can have money, but we should be very careful not to love it. St Paul goes on to tell Timothy how to help the rich:

As for the rich of this world, charge them not to be haughty, not to set their hopes on uncertain riches but on God who richly furnishes us with everything to enjoy. They are to do good, to be rich in good deeds, liberal and generous, thus laying up for themselves a good foundation for the future, so that they may take hold of the life which is life indeed (*1 Tim* 6:17-19).

St Athanasius of Alexandria, a fourth-century bishop and theologian, makes clear that the things of this world are worth nothing in comparison with those of the next life:

> Let us not think that those who despise the world are making a great sacrifice, because the whole world is worth very little in comparison with heaven. Therefore, even if we owned the whole world and renounced it, we would not be doing anything worthy by comparison with the kingdom of heaven (*Catena Aurea*, Vol. VI, p. 311).

Detachment of the heart

In all this, it is a matter of having our heart detached from the things of this world, even though we may be wealthy by the world's standards. That is to say, we can have things and use and enjoy them, but we should not have our heart in them. St Francis de Sales, a seventeenth-century bishop of Geneva, gives a good analogy:

> Pharmacists keep almost every kind of poison in stock for use on various occasions, yet they are not themselves poisoned, because they merely have it in their shops and not in their bodies. So also, you can possess riches without being poisoned by them if you merely keep them in your home and purse and not in your heart" (*Introduction to the Devout Life*, III, 14).

St John of the Cross, a sixteenth-century monk in the Carmelite order, goes further to warn that attachment to material things can lead to lowering oneself so as to be equal to those things, and even to being lower, to serving them:

> It ought to be kept in mind that an attachment to a

creature makes a person equal to that creature; the firmer the attachment, the closer is the likeness to the creature, and the greater the equality. For love effects a likeness between the lover and the object loved. As a result, David said of those who set their hearts upon their idols: "Let all who set their hearts on them become like them" (Ps 113:8). He who loves a creature, then, is as low as that creature, and in some way even lower, because love not only equates, but even subjects the lover to the loved object (*The Ascent of Mount Carmel*, Bk 1, Ch 4, 3).

We see the truth of this, for example, in those who have bought a new car or some other expensive object, and then spend great amounts of time washing and polishing it to keep it in pristine condition. Instead of being the master of their goods, they become their servant. Returning to what really matters in life, St John of the Cross says:

> All the wealth and glory of creation compared with the wealth that is God is utter poverty and misery in the Lord's sight. The person who loves and possesses these things is completely poor and miserable before God and will be unable to attain the richness and glory of the state of transformation in God; the miserable and poor is extremely distant from the supremely rich and glorious" (*ibid.*, 7).

The dangers of love of wealth

There is a big difference between having wealth but being detached from it and generous in using it for the benefit of others, and being greedy with it. Pope St Paul VI, in his encyclical letter *Populorum progressio* (1967), warns strongly about the dangers of the latter:

> Increased possessions are not the ultimate goal of nations nor of individuals. All growth is ambivalent. It is essential if man is to develop as a man, but in a way it imprisons man if he considers it the supreme good, and it restricts his vision. Then we see hearts harden and minds close, and men no longer gather together in friendship but out of self-interest, which soon leads to oppositions and disunity. The exclusive pursuit of possessions thus becomes an obstacle to individual fulfilment and to man's true greatness. Both for nations and for individual men, avarice is the most evident form of moral underdevelopment (n. 19).

Another way of life

Pope Francis, in his encyclical letter *Laudato si'* proposes a completely different way to live:

> Christian spirituality proposes an alternative understanding of the quality of life, and encourages a prophetic and contemplative lifestyle, one capable of deep enjoyment free of the obsession with consumption. We need to take up an ancient lesson, found in different religious traditions and also in the Bible. It is the conviction that "less is more". A constant flood of new consumer goods can baffle the heart and prevent us from cherishing each thing and each moment.
>
> To be serenely present to each reality, however small it may be, opens us to much greater horizons of under-

standing and personal fulfilment. Christian spirituality proposes a growth marked by moderation and the capacity to be happy with little. It is a return to that simplicity which allows us to stop and appreciate the small things, to be grateful for the opportunities which life affords us, to be spiritually detached from what we possess, and not to succumb to sadness for what we lack. This implies avoiding the dynamic of dominion and the mere accumulation of pleasures (n. 222).

This way of living is possible for everyone, even those with considerable wealth. It is a matter of detachment of the heart from material things, of putting the heart rather into the things of God and of the persons around us, especially members of our family. Then we will enjoy more the simple things of life: the family gatherings, the walks in the countryside, the time in the garden… And, as Pope Francis says, not to succumb to sadness for what we lack, for what our neighbours have and we do not. Pope Francis goes on:

> Such sobriety, when lived freely and consciously, is liberating. It is not a lesser life or one lived with less intensity. On the contrary, it is a way of living life to the full. In reality, those who enjoy more and live better each moment are those who have given up dipping here and there, always on the look-out for what they do not have. They experience what it means to appreciate each person and each thing, learning familiarity with the simplest things and how to enjoy them. So they are able to shed unsatisfied needs, reducing their obsessiveness and weariness. Even living on little, they can

> live a lot, above all when they cultivate other pleasures and find satisfaction in fraternal encounters, in service, in developing their gifts, in music and art, in contact with nature, in prayer. Happiness means knowing how to limit some needs which only diminish us, and being open to the many different possibilities which life can offer (*Laudato si'*, n. 223).

In our consumerist society, we do well to listen to this wise advice and to find the way to enjoy the little things of life without being obsessed with the accumulation of more and more goods.

In an address to a conference on natality on 10 May 2024, Pope Francis warns of another consequence of an excessively materialistic society: it's effect on birth rates.

> In the past, there was no lack of studies and theories warning about the number of inhabitants on earth, because the birth of too many children would have created economic imbalances, a lack of resources, and pollution. I was always struck by how these theses, now long outdated, spoke of *human beings* as if they were problems. But human life is not a problem, it is a gift.
>
> And at the root of pollution and starvation in the world are not children being born, but the choices of those who think only of themselves, the delirium of an unbridled, blind and rampant materialism, of a consumerism that, like an evil virus, undermines the existence of people and society at the root.
>
> The problem is not *how many of us there are in the world*, but *the world that we are building* – this is the

problem; not children, but selfishness, which creates injustice and structures of sin, to the point of weaving unhealthy interdependencies between social, economic and political systems.

Selfishness makes us deaf to the voice of God, who loves first and teaches how to love, and to the voice of our brothers and sisters beside us; it anaesthetises the heart, it makes us live through objects, no longer understanding why; it induces us to have many goods, while no longer knowing how to do good. And houses fill up with objects and are emptied of children, becoming very sad places There is no shortage of dogs and cats… These are not lacking. There is a shortage of children. The problem of our world is not the children who are born: it is selfishness, consumerism and individualism, which make people satiated, lonely and unhappy.

Generosity with our wealth

Wealth, when all is said and done, is a good thing. If everyone has some, they will not have to go hungry or worry about paying bills or about the future. They will be able to provide for the needs of their family and be able to help others. There will always be people who have less, and those with more will be able to come to their assistance. In so doing, they will be storing up treasure in heaven, knowing that whatever they did for others, they were doing for Christ himself. And they will deserve an eternal reward. He said so: "Come, O blessed of my Father, inherit the kingdom prepared for you from the foundation of the world; for I was hungry and you gave me food, I was thirsty and you gave me to drink, I was a stranger and you welcomed me, I was naked and you clothed me..." (*Matt* 25: 34-36).

St Basil the Great, a fourth-century bishop and theologian, is very clear on this:

> Now you are going to leave your money behind you here whether you like it or not, but on the other hand you will be taking with you to the Lord the credit obtained for your good works. All who are standing round the judge of all men will hail you helper and generous benefactor and will use of you all the names that imply kindness and humanity. Don't you see those men who lavish their wealth on theatrical shows or boxing or wrestling contests, or mimes or shows where men fight with wild beasts, things one would disdain even to look at, and all for short-lived honours, for the shouts and applause of the people? And will you be stingy in spending money when so great a glory will be your reward? ... Come then, scatter abroad your riches, be liberal and magnanimous in giving to the poor. Let it be said of you too: 'He has distributed freely, he has given to the poor, his righteousness endures forever' (*On charity*, 3, 6).

On the other hand, St Basil is scathing in his indictment of those who have wealth but refuse to help others with it:

> Now indeed you show yourself sullen and access to you is scarcely possible while you refuse to meet anyone for fear you might be compelled to let even a scrap slip through your fingers. You only know one phrase: 'I'm a poor man, I've nothing to give.' Yes, you really are a

poor man, without riches of any sort; poor in affection, poor in humanity, poor in faith in God, poor in eternal hope (*ibid.*).

The lesson is clear. We can have wealth, but we should not be attached to it. And we should be generous in helping others with it. In any case, no matter how much we have, we cannot take it with us. Jesus has a stern warning for those who are too attached to their wealth:

> Take heed, and beware of all covetousness; for a man's life does not consist in the abundance of his possessions. And he told them a parable, saying, "The land of a rich man brought forth plentifully; and he thought to himself, 'What shall I do, for I have nowhere to store my crops?' And he said, 'I will do this: I will pull down my barns and build larger ones; and there I will store all my grain and my goods. And I will say to my soul, Soul, you have ample goods laid up for many years; take your ease, eat, drink, be merry.' But God said to him, "Fool! This night your soul is required of you; and the things you have prepared, whose will they be?" So is he who lays up treasure for himself, and is not rich toward God (*Luke* 12:15-21).

7

Striving to please God

When all is said and done, what we are really trying to do with our life in order to deserve to spend eternity with God in heaven is to do what pleases him. Again, our relationship with God is very much like our relationship with our parents. We want to treat them well, because they love us and put themselves out for us. If we love them, we naturally want to make them happy, to show them with deeds that we love them. And we do this by striving to do what pleases them.

It is the same with God, who is our Father. Except that in our relationship with him, there is more at stake. Eternal life, to be exact, which is the very purpose of our life on earth. If we don't succeed in making it to heaven when we die, our whole life will have been an abject failure. We might have made a lot of money, achieved a certain fame, made some contribution to society, but if we don't go to heaven, everything else will be meaningless. We will have squandered our short life on earth and missed out on eternal life with God.

What does it mean to do what pleases God? Simply, to do what he is asking of us, to do his will. Throughout the day, and throughout our life. This is not difficult. God does not ask of us something that we are incapable of doing. He knows each of us better than we know ourselves, and he only asks us to do what we are capable of doing. And he gives us the grace, the help, to do it.

As I explained in my book *The Final Exam – Preparing for the Judgment* in the final chapter, we will all be judged differently, in keeping with the gifts and talents and opportunities God has given to each one. He has given more to some than to others, and he can ask more from them than from others. But even when we asks more, it is because he has given them more, and it is no more difficult for them to respond to his requests than it is for a person who has been given less.

Listening to our conscience

How do we know what God is asking of us? Our conscience is the best guide. We all have a conscience, and it is nothing more than the judgments we make throughout the day about what is right and wrong, about what God is asking of us in each moment. The first such judgment each day may be simply to get out of bed when our alarm goes off and to start the day. If we stay in bed, our conscience will accuse us of being lazy and lacking in will power. In another moment it will be to treat the members of our family well, to leave for work on time, to be honest in work, to leave work in order to arrive home and have dinner with our family...

To use a Christian concept, to do the will of God is to seek holiness. St Alphonsus Liguori says that all of holiness consists in the love of God, and all the love of God consists in doing his will. Again, we can understand this by looking at how we relate to our parents. If we really love them, we will try to do what pleases them, to do what they are asking of us. Not to do that is to show them that we do not really care, that we do not really love them.

Jesus himself tells us this: "As the Father has loved me, so have I loved you; abide in my love. If you keep my commandments, you will abide in my love, just as I have kept my Father's commandments and abide in his love" (*John* 15:9-10).

Other voices

Knowing what God is asking of us requires that we listen to him, that we be attentive to what he is telling us throughout the day. Sometimes we can find this hard. The reason is that we often hear other voices conflicting with the voice of God. And sometimes they are very much louder. For example, suppose we are working at something we are supposed to do, like writing a report at the office, or doing the ironing at home. Then suddenly we have the urge to check the news or the messages on our phone, and this in turn can lead to following up by looking at a YouTube clip on an interesting topic. Hours later we might still be there, wasting time on something we should not have begun at all. What has happened is that, in addition to the voice of God telling us to continue with our work, we are hearing a much louder, more appealing, voice suggesting that we just take a brief break and check our mobile phone. Only for a few minutes, of course. But then...

The reality is that the voice of our whims, of our love of comfort, of pleasure, can drown out the voice of God. This can happen often. We all have the experience. There are two rules of thumb to distinguish between the voice of God and the other voices that might lead us astray. The first one is simple. The voice of God is the softer voice. This is understandable. Fulfilling our duty by doing the will of God is often far less appealing than following the whim to entertain ourselves or pop something into our mouth by way of a snack. So, if there are two voices in conflict with each other, and one of them is to fulfil a duty while the other is to do something more enjoyable, clearly the softer voice, the call to duty, must be coming from God.

The other rule of thumb is that the voice of God is the less appealing of the two voices. Again, the voice of pleasure, of comfort, is always more appealing than the call to fulfil a duty which God is asking of us.

In this area, some people are completely out of control and others have enough love for God and self-control to do what God wants of them. At least most of the time. We do well to examine ourselves on this point to see where we are on this spectrum. We would all like to be strong-willed people who have their lives in order, who do what they ought instead of what they feel like doing at the time. In simple terms, to be people of will and not of whim.

The jigsaw puzzle of life

A big help in doing what God is asking instead of what we feel like doing is to look at the whole of our life as if it were a giant jigsaw puzzle. Really, it is. God has a beautiful picture in mind for each one of us. Everyone's picture is unique, very different from the others, because each one of us is unique. The finished picture of our life will be different from that of everyone else.

But there are two major differences between the jigsaw puzzle of life and that of an ordinary jigsaw puzzle. First, we don't know what the finished picture of our life will look like. When we buy a jigsaw puzzle, we can see the finished picture on the cover of the box, and then we put the pieces in place to match the picture. With our life, especially when we are young and just starting out, we have no idea what the final picture will look like.

Second, with the puzzle we buy, we know how many pieces it

has: 500, 1000, even 2000. We can then adjust our rate of work accordingly. We know it will take a long time to put 2000 pieces in place, so we don't get impatient if our progress is slow. But with the jigsaw puzzle of life, we have no idea how many pieces it has. We usually assume it will have the many pieces that correspond to the average life expectancy of someone born when we were. But we can't be sure we will live that long. Many people's lives are unexpectedly cut short, through sickness, heart attacks, accidents… So it is very important always to make the effort to put in place all the pieces, and the right pieces, that God wants for that day. For all we know, that day may be our last.

Throughout the day we are putting pieces in place. Every time we start a new activity, we place another piece. We can put the piece that God wants us to put there or some other piece. If it is the one he wants, it will blend in with those around it and form part of a beautiful picture. If it is not, it will stand out as the wrong piece and it will not match the others.

Only at the end of our life will we see the finished picture. It can be the one God planned for us if we always put in place the pieces he wants. Or it can be a discordant mismatch of pieces without any beauty, without any harmony. In the judgment, we will see our picture, every aspect of it. And God will reward us more if our picture more closely matches the one he planned for us.

Even if we make a mistake and put the wrong piece, we can tell God we are sorry and strive to make up for it, especially by struggling to avoid doing it again. Then God, in his wisdom and mercy, can in some way cover over the mistake, so that the finished picture is not as unseemly as it would otherwise have been.

In this way, we can see our daily life as a challenge. A challenge to put in place the pieces of our puzzle that God wants, by doing his will. Then we can look forward to seeing the finished picture in the judgment when we die.

In this struggle we will be helped greatly by developing some important virtues, good habits, that help us do what God is asking of us. That is our next topic.

8

GROWING IN VIRTUES

We all have a general sense of what virtues are. The word is attractive, and a person with virtues is attractive too. That person lives a better life, does what they ought to do instead of what they feel like doing at the time, gets things done, is more kind and generous…

Really, we can see what a virtue is by comparing it with its opposite, a vice. In simple terms, a virtue is a good habit that facilitates the doing of good, whereas a vice is a bad habit that facilitates doing what is wrong. And so we have such virtues as charity, industriousness, honesty, cheerfulness, kindness, and so on. And we have vices such as laziness, selfishness, pride, dishonesty and self-indulgence.

We could dedicate the rest of this book, and other books besides, to consider the various virtues. But let us limit ourselves here to consider four important ones that the ancients called cardinal virtues. They are prudence, justice, fortitude and temperance. The word cardinal comes from the Latin word *cardo*, meaning hinge. Other virtues hang off the cardinal virtues just as a door hangs on its hinge.

The book of Wisdom in the Bible mentions these four virtues: "… for she teaches self-control and prudence, justice and courage" (*Wis* 8:7). And philosophers like Aristotle wrote about them.

We are not born with virtues. Yes, we may have a natural tendency to be orderly, thoughtful of others, hardworking, etc., but we still need to struggle to grow in these areas so that we fix these tendencies more firmly in our whole way of being, so that they become habits,

virtues. And we can also grow in virtues for which we do not have a natural tendency. That is to say, we can acquire virtues. This we do by making a conscious effort to practise them, repeating over and over again the acts that will develop into firm habits.

The cardinal virtues are especially important in helping us do what God is asking of us, instead of what we feel like doing at the time. Thus, they assist us in having self-mastery and joy in living the good life that will enable us to be better people here on earth, and to make it easier to reach the ultimate goal of eternal life with God in heaven.

Prudence

The first of the cardinal virtues is prudence. It is often defined as the virtue which helps us discern our true good in every circumstance and to choose the right means of achieving it. From this definition we can see how important prudence is. When we are wondering what we ought to do in a given moment, prudence helps us know what our true good is and to choose the right means to achieve it. It helps us discern between what we feel like doing and what is our true good, what God is asking of us. It is sometimes called the charioteer of the virtues for it guides the other virtues to their proper end, as the charioteer guides the horses to pull the chariot in the desired direction.

It is prudence that guides the judgment of our conscience, helping us to discern and choose what God is asking of us. The prudent person is not guided by whims or feelings, but rather by the will of God in that moment. Prudence helps us apply general moral principles to individual cases or circumstances correctly and thus to overcome doubts about how to act. With this virtue, we will more readily see what God is asking of us and we will do it, thus speeding us on our way to heaven.

We can grow in prudence by pondering carefully what God is asking of us at the time and choosing that, by consulting others before deciding, etc. At the same time, we should avoid acting impulsively without thinking, changing our mind suddenly when we have considered carefully beforehand what is the right course of action, not consulting someone who can help us because we fear they will not give us the advice we want to hear, etc.

Justice

Justice can be described briefly as the firm will to give to each one his due. It refers both to giving to God what is owed him, like our worship, our prayer, obedience to his will, etc., and to giving to our neighbour what is owed him, like paying our lawful debts, paying just wages, returning borrowed property, respecting our neighbour's property, etc. St Paul makes very clear why we should live this virtue: "Masters, treat your servants justly and fairly, knowing that you also have a Master in heaven" (*Col* 4:1). Again, we can see how important this virtue is in doing the will of God and deserving eternal life with him.

We can grow in justice by making the effort to discern what is right in each circumstance and then carry it out. Sometimes dishonesty may appear more attractive and more profitable, but we should always choose what we know to be right.

Fortitude

When we considered how easily we give in to our whims and feelings instead of doing what God is asking, we see the need for will power, or fortitude. It is sometimes also called courage. We can define fortitude as the virtue that ensures firmness in difficulties and constancy in the pursuit of the good. That is, this virtue relates especially to choices we must make that involve doing something difficult, and it gives us the strength to overcome the difficulty in the pursuit of the good. The more fortitude we have, the easier it will be to do what God is asking of us. This virtue helps us to be strong in resisting temptations to sin and in doing what is right, no matter how difficult it may be. In its ultimate degree, fortitude helps someone overcome fear, even fear of death, in standing up for the faith and for what is right. The many martyrs of the early centuries and of the present time had fortitude to defend their faith and virtue. They did this by relying on God as their strength: "The Lord is my strength and my song; he has become my salvation" (*Psalm* 118:14).

We can grow in fortitude by doing little things each day that cost us but that we know are right, like getting out of bed on time in the morning, starting our work, tackling the difficult jobs, denying ourselves in certain foods, etc.

Temperance

Another extremely important virtue in helping us do what pleases God and not what pleases ourselves is temperance. It is the virtue that moderates the attraction of pleasures and provides balance in the use of created goods. We are naturally drawn to what is pleasurable and to seek pleasures to excess, and so we need the virtue of temperance to hold us back and to do what is right in the circumstance. God wants us to enjoy the pleasures of life, and for this reason he gave us our senses of taste, smell, hearing, seeing and touch. But he wants us to enjoy these pleasures with moderation, lest we end up indulging ourselves without any self-control. Temperance is called sobriety in the pleasures of drink, chastity in the pleasures of the flesh, and abstinence in the pleasures of eating. One might say that temperance is like the reins that the rider uses to hold the horse back, and fortitude is like the spurs to spur the horse on.

How can we grow in temperance? Simply by controlling our impulse to satiate ourselves excessively in the pleasures of life. For example, controlling our use of the mobile phone and television, not eating more than we need, taking care in chastity not to watch television programs or films that do not respect the dignity of the human person, avoiding excessive drinking of alcohol, etc. As with all virtues, the more we practise self-control by living temperance, the easier it will become. Then we will find it easier to do what pleases God, and the easier it will be to set off firmly on the way to heaven.

9

Obstacles along the way

It would be nice if we saw clearly the goal of eternity with God in heaven, and we grew in virtues to strengthen us on the way there, so that our journey was practically without difficulties. But that is not case. For anyone. We all face difficulties in life and, in a sense, they make our struggle to please God more meritorious. Perhaps Christ was alluding to this when he said: "From the days of John the Baptist until now the kingdom of heaven has suffered violence, and men of violence take it by force" (*Matt* 11:12). Yes, we all have to battle our way into heaven.

It is a bit like paddling a canoe upstream. The current is against us and if we stop paddling, we will soon be drifting backwards. At different times in history and in different places the current has been stronger or weaker. Right now, in most of the Western world, the anti-Christian, anti-moral, anti-God, hedonistic current is very strong. It has never been easy to live a good life and make our way to heaven, but right now it is harder. At the same time, we have the help, the grace of God to strengthen us for the journey.

For the sake of simplicity, we can divide the difficulties we are going to meet into three categories: the world, the flesh and the devil. For this purpose, we can consider that the world represents everything outside of us, the environment of the society in which we live. The flesh is everything inside us: the wayward tendencies of original sin. And the devil is the devil, Satan, "who prowls around like a roaring lion, seeking someone to devour" (*1 Peter* 5:8).

The world

It is no secret that these days it is difficult to be a good person, to stand up to the many forces in society trying to drag us down, to hold us back. To see these forces, all we need to do is turn on the television or the internet and see the immorality, the pornography, the lack of values that abounds, especially at night. Or talk with our colleagues of work or our neighbours, and see their attitude to sex, to marital fidelity, to the right to life of the unborn child, to the dignity of the elderly, to the worship of God, even to honesty.

Okay, that is true. But we can face this situation with two possible attitudes. Either remain silent, go along with it and compromise our own standards in order to be accepted by others. Or challenge these values, standing up for what we believe is right and helping change the world for the better. The first is the easy way, but we all know it is not the right way. It is to capitulate, to reinforce the wrong ideas and therefore contribute to the moral decline.

The second is to stand up and fight for what is right and good. Fortunately, there are a good number of people who are doing this. They are criticised for their beliefs, which many consider frightfully old-fashioned and out of touch. But they don't care. They have the courage to stand up for what they know is right. And little by little they help others to see the wisdom of what they stand for and to follow them. Together, they make the world a better place.

We can recall the wise words of Edmund Burke, the eighteenth-century Irish statesman and political philosopher: "All that is necessary for the triumph of evil is that the good do nothing". Or those other words, "Nobody makes a greater mistake than he who did nothing because he could only do a little".

This reminds me of the story I once heard of an old man walking along the beach at dawn and noticing a boy ahead of him picking up starfish stranded on the sand and throwing them into the sea. When he asked the boy why he was doing this, the boy answered that the starfish would die if left until the sun struck them. The man then pointed out that the beach went on for miles and there were starfish as far as the eye could see. He asked the boy whether he thought what he was doing would make any difference. The boy looked at the starfish in his hand, threw it to the safety of the waves and said: "It makes a difference to this one."

Back in the fifth century, in answer to those who said that the times in which people lived were very difficult, St Augustine answered: "Let us live well and the times will be good. We are the times; as we live, so the times will be" (*Sermon* 80, 8).

And towards the end of the nineteenth century, Pope Leo XIII wrote: "To recoil before an enemy, or to keep silent when from all sides such clamours are raised against the truth, is the part of a man either devoid of character or who entertains doubt as to the truth of what he professes to believe. In both cases such a mode of behaving is base and is insulting to God, and both are incompatible with the salvation of mankind" (*Sapientiae Christianae*, 1889).

In answer to those who say that the Church is out of touch with the times, one could answer that it is rather the times that are out of touch with the Church, with the teachings of Jesus Christ, who is "the way, the truth and the life" (*John* 14:6). It is up to us to make those teachings more widely known, and to stand up for them, so that others will come to see that they are what is truly good for society, for families and for individuals.

And, of course, at the same time we have to struggle to avoid the most hostile influences in society, on the internet and television, in the cinema, in conversations with certain people…

The flesh

As if doing battle with the hostile environment around us weren't enough, we also have to contend with the tendencies of original sin within us. These tendencies are common to all of us. They incline us to act in certain ways which are at least inappropriate, and sometimes sinful. They have been likened to faulty wheel alignment in a car. Unless the driver grips the steering wheel tightly in order to compensate, the car will veer off course. We can consider them in their effect on the intellect, the will and the two sense appetites. These tendencies leave us wounded, but not corrupted.

In the *intellect*, or mind, we have the defect of *pride*, which is an exaggerated sense of self-worth. We all suffer from it, in various degrees and ways. We tend to think ourselves better than we really are, to think ourselves better than those around us, to resent criticism and think it unjustified, to make excuses when criticised, to make sure everyone around us knows of our accomplishments, to be sad and envious when someone else has something we don't have, etc. St Josemaría Escrivá once commented that the best business in the world would be to buy people for what they are worth and sell them for what they think they are worth! (cf. *Cartas* 1. n. 36) And we all know how repugnant a proud, vain, person is.

Because pride affects the intellect, by which we understand and judge reality, it is difficult to see it, especially in ourselves. It affects our very way of seeing ourselves. A helpful analogy is that pride is like yellow-coloured sunglasses, which make everything look brighter than it is in fact. When we take off the glasses, we see things as they really are. But in the case of pride, we can't take off the sunglasses. They are built in, they affect the very way we look on ourselves. It is as if someone drew some yellow lines on a piece of white paper and we looked at them through yellow sunglasses. We couldn't see the yellow lines.

The antidote to pride is of course humility, that true appraisal of our self-worth. St Teresa of Avila said that humility is to walk in the truth. And the truth is that along with our many virtues and talents, we also have many defects and sins. Just as it is helpful to acknowledge our many good qualities, so we can thank God for them, so it also helpful to recognise our many failings, so that we can struggle to overcome them. If we live humility, we will never think how good we are, or how well we have done, as if we did it by ourselves. Really, everything we are and everything we do is God's work. Humility helps us to thank God for everything. If proud people are repugnant, humble people are pleasant and much appreciated.

So important is this virtue that St Augustine once said: "If you ask me what is the most essential thing in the religion and in the discipline of Jesus Christ, I will answer that the first thing is humility, the second is humility and the third is humility." This great saint also humbly acknowledged his own weakness: "There is no sin or crime committed by another man that I am not capable of committing myself, given my weakness, and if until now I have not committed it, it is because God, in his mercy, has not allowed it and has kept me in the good" (*Confessions*, 2, 7).

An outstanding example of humility in recent times was Mother St Teresa of Calcutta. In an interview with *Time* magazine in December 1989 she was asked if she felt she had no special qualities. Her answer was simple: "I don't think so. I don't claim anything of the work. I am like a little pencil in God's hand. That is all. He does the thinking. He does the writing. The pencil has nothing to do with it. The pencil has only to allow itself to be used. In human terms, the success of our work should not have happened, no?" St John Vianney, the Cure of Ars, sums it up: "My children, we are in reality only what we are in the eyes of God, and nothing more."

If in the intellect we have the defect of pride, which gives us an exaggerated sense of self-worth, in the *will* we have *self-love* or *selfishness, self-centredness*. Again, we all have this tendency, some more, some less. We all tend naturally to think of ourselves first, of what we would like, of how we feel, of what we would like others to do for us. And we complain if they don't ask us how we are, they don't notice that we are especially tired or sick, they don't help us finish a job, they don't thank us for a favour we have done them … Like pride, self-love makes us unpleasant, unappealing to others.

The virtue that counteracts self-love is charity. The more we live charity, in the sense of loving others, thinking first of them, asking them how they are, putting ourselves out for them, etc., the less self-centred we will be and the more appreciated by others. When we think about it, we probably all know people who distinguish themselves by their self-centredness, and others who are very kind, thoughtful, generous. We want to be one of the latter. But this takes effort.

A good start is to think of someone we know, or have read about, who is known for their self-giving to others, their generosity, and then strive to imitate them. They might be someone from the Bible, like Jesus Christ or the Blessed Virgin Mary, or someone from our own time, like Mother Teresa of Calcutta, St John Paul II or someone from our extended family or our neighbourhood.

Jesus Christ is always a good model. After all, he was God, God in human flesh. He was perfect God and perfect man. And, as St John writes in his Gospel, "Now before the feast of the Passover, when Jesus knew that his hour had come to depart out of this world to the Father, having loved his own who were in the world, he loved them to the end" (*John* 13:1). St John goes on to relate how, in the course of the Last Supper with his apostles, Jesus washed the feet of the apostles, a task normally done by a servant. He then invited them: "If I then, your Lord and Teacher, have washed your feet you also ought to wash one another's feet. For I have given you an example, that you also should do as I have done to you" (*John* 13:14-15). From the Last Supper Jesus went out to begin his suffering and death for mankind.

Before he went out, he told the apostles, "A new commandment I give to you, that you love one another; even as I have loved you, that you also love one another. By this all men will know that you are my disciples, if you have love for one another" (*John* 13:34-35). And a little later, "Greater love has no man than this, that a man lay down his life for his friends" (*John* 15:13). Jesus laid down his life for all mankind, to redeem them and open the gates of heaven for them, and he wants all of us to be ready to give of ourselves to those around us.

This is demanding, of course, but very beneficial for all concerned. Beneficial for ourselves, when we put ourselves out for others, and beneficial for those others. Charity begins at home. After all, those who have the first claim on our love are those closest to us. Our self-giving here can take the form of spending more time with our spouse or children, helping someone who needs that help at a given time, offering to drive someone to a game, class, or medical appointment, staying up with a sick child at night, etc. It is when we put ourselves out for them that they appreciate that we really love them, and our love for them grows accordingly.

After the family, our love for others can be shown in our extended family, our workplace, our neighbourhood. We all know people who are very generous and kind in those places, and we can be one of them. It might be just a smile, a kind word or an enquiry as to how they are feeling. Or something more generous, like driving them home from work, making a meal for their family when their husband or wife is sick, etc.

An inspiring example of self-giving to others was Mother Teresa of Calcutta. In a talk in Rome in October 1984, she related this story:

> One day they brought a man from the streets and half of his body was all eaten up; worms were crawling all over his body, and nobody could stand near him, the odour was so great. So I went to clean him and he looked at me, and then he asked: "Why do you do this? Everybody has given me away. Why do you do this? Why do you come near me?" "I love you", I said. "I love you. You are Jesus in a distressing disguise. Jesus is sharing his passion with you." And he looked up at me and said, "And you – you too, by doing what you are doing, are sharing." I said, "No, I am sharing the joy of loving with you. I love the Jesus in you." And this Hindu gentleman, so full of suffering, what did he say? "Glory be to Jesus Christ." There was no complaint

of those big worms eating into his body. There was no crying, no calling. He realised that he was somebody, that he was loved.

This was Mother Teresa. Always giving, always loving, seeing Jesus Christ in the "poorest of the poor", as she called them. In so doing, she was helping others realise that they were somebody, that they were loved. It didn't make any difference whether they had an odour coming from an unwashed and decaying body, whether they were Christian or Hindu. They were human beings and she poured herself out for them. We store up great treasure in heaven when we give of ourselves to others as she did.

After considering the two spiritual powers of the soul, the intellect and will, where we find the wayward tendencies of pride and selfishness, we come to the two sense appetites, which are more aligned with our bodily nature. They are what are called the irascible appetite, which seeks goods which are difficult or unpleasant, and the concupiscible appetite, which seeks pleasurable goods. Forgive me for using this perhaps unusual terminology, but it is the customary one. Again, in the sense appetites we find wayward tendencies brought about by original sin.

Beginning with the *irascible appetite*, it is no secret that some of the goods or goals we all pursue are more difficult, more challenging, and they involve an element of sacrifice. Think, for example, of the goods of raising children from infancy to adulthood, of holding a marriage together in good times and in bad, of holding down a job and advancing in it, of obtaining a high school or higher degree, or simply of staying fit and healthy. These are all obvious, even necessary, goods but pursuing them is not easy.

In all of these areas we have the natural tendency, as an effect of original sin, to give up, to convince ourselves that we can't do it, that it is too hard, that it is not worthwhile anyway. We call this tendency by different names: *laziness, softness, lack of will power, inconstancy*. It would be good if we always found these endeavours easy and enjoyable, but that is simply not the case. Yet we must pursue them.

In this area we need a virtue which we have already considered: fortitude, or courage. The way to grow in it is to be constant, persevering, demanding on ourselves in fulfilling our duties. The more we push ourselves, the stronger and more effective we become. We sometimes surprise even ourselves at how much we have achieved, especially when it has been difficult. At the end of our life, we can then look back and give thanks that we didn't give up, that we achieved so much.

Conversely, we can convince ourselves that it is too hard, or not worthwhile, and throw in the towel. We can stay in bed instead of getting up when we ought, put off starting that difficult job, leave the job half done, stay at work instead of coming home to our family, hole ourselves up in our own room instead of spending time with our spouse and children. It is up to each one of us to decide which way we want to go. In short, we can be a failure or a big success.

Naturally, even those who achieve a lot will fail some of the time. We are not superheroes who always succeed. But even our lapses, our failures, can spur us on to start over, to try harder. Then our victories are all the more meritorious.

In the other sense appetite, the *concupiscible*, which seeks the pleasurable good, we have the natural tendency to *overindulge ourselves, to seek too much pleasure*, to lose our self-control. We all experience this. We eat too much of foods we like, drink too much alcohol, spend too much time looking at our mobile phone, watching television, surfing the net or looking at social media, staring lustfully at attractive women or men, seeking the pleasures of sex in inappropriate ways ... We lack impulse control.

To counteract this tendency, we need another virtue we have already considered: temperance. As we saw, in the area of the pleasures of life, we need to hold ourselves back, to moderate our search for pleasure, as the rider uses the reins to hold the horse back. Again, it is up to each one of us to decide how we want to live. We can simply let ourselves go and be incapable of controlling our desire for pleasure. There are many people like this. All those suffering from addictions know what it is like. But even short of addictions, there are many who lack temperance in one area or another. Apart from the evil of the sins that many commit in this area, even from a human point of view it is obvious that people who have their appetites under control are more balanced, more effective persons. Let us decide to be one of them.

So much is this common sense, that ancient writers spoke of it in the same terms. Consider, for example, Cicero (106-43BC):

> But it is essential to every inquiry about duty that we keep before our eyes how far superior man is by nature to cattle and other beasts... And if we will only bear in mind the superiority and dignity of our nature, we shall realise how wrong it is to abandon ourselves to excess and to live in luxury and voluptuousness, and how right it is to live in thrift, self-denial, simplicity, and sobriety (*On Duties*, Harvard University Press, Cambridge 1913, 107-109).

By way of summing up, St Paul speaks of the spiritual struggle against our wayward tendencies, contrasting living according to the flesh with living according to the Spirit. He writes to the Church in Galatia:

> Now the works of the flesh are plain: immorality, impurity, licentiousness, idolatry, sorcery, enmity, strife, jealousy, anger, selfishness, dissension, party spirit, envy, drunkenness, carousing, and the like. I warn you as I warned you before, that those who do such things shall not inherit the kingdom of God. But the fruit of the Spirit is love, joy, peace, patience, kindness, goodness, faithfulness, gentleness, self-control; against such there is no law (*Gal* 5:19-23).

This reminds me of a story, with the same theme and an important conclusion, often told by Wayne Bennett, one of Australia's greatest Rugby League coaches.

> An old Cherokee is teaching his grandson about life. "A fight is going on inside me", he says to the boy. "It's a terrible fight, and it's between two wolves. One is evil: he is anger, envy, sorrow, regret, greed, arrogance, self-pity, guilt, resentment, inferiority, lies, false pride superiority and ego. The other is good: he is joy, peace, love, hope, serenity, humility, kindness, benevolence, empathy, generosity, truth, compassion and faith. The same fight is going on inside you – and inside every other person, too."

> The grandson thinks about it for a minute and then asks his grandfather, "Which wolf will win?" The old Cherokee simply replies, "The one you feed."

There is a lot of wisdom in this story. We can feed the evil tendencies by giving in to them repeatedly and then they will dominate. Or we can struggle to overcome them and strive to live joy, peace, love and kindness, and so be the good person we want to be. It is up to us.

The devil

As if everything we have just considered about the obstacles we will encounter on our way to heaven weren't enough, we have the added obstacle of the devil. The devil is an angel created by God at the beginning of time, who rebelled against God and now finds himself forever separated from him and in the fires of hell. He is allowed to act on earth and he does everything he can to tempt us to sin, to prevent us from getting close to God and being with him forever in heaven.

The devil is real. In the Lord's Prayer Jesus taught us to pray: "but deliver us from evil". The *Catechism of the Catholic Church* explains: "In this petition, evil is not an abstraction, but refers to a person, Satan, the Evil One, the angel who opposes God. The devil (dia-bolos) is the one who 'throws himself across' God's plan and his work of salvation accomplished in Christ" (*CCC* 2851). The very name of the devil in Greek, *diabolos*, from which we have the word diabolical, means to throw across, to divide. The devil throws himself across God's plan of salvation by dividing people from God and from one another. Wherever there is division, the devil is at work. We see this division in families, in workplaces, in countries and in international relations.

Quoting the Scriptures, the Catechism goes on to speak of the devil in graphic terms: "'A murderer from the beginning, … a liar and the father of lies,' Satan is 'the deceiver of the whole world.' Through him sin and death entered the world and by his definitive defeat all creation will be 'freed from the corruption of sin and death' *(CCC* 2852; *John* 8:44; Rev 12:9; *Roman Missal,* Eucharistic Prayer IV).

Jesus himself prays to the Father to protect us from the devil: "I do not pray that you should take them out of the world, but that you should keep them from the evil one" *(John* 17:15). Jesus doesn't ask the Father to take us out of the world. After all, we belong in the world, we live in it and we are here to change it for the better. Jesus does pray that we do not give in to the temptations of the devil.

Pope Francis has spoken about the devil numerous times from the very beginning of his pontificate. In his Wednesday audience on 27 December 2023, after talking about how the devil deceived Adam and Eve in the garden, as related in the book of Genesis, he went on to say:

> Dear brothers and sisters, one must never dialogue with the devil. Never! You should never enter into conversation [with him]. Jesus never dialogued with the devil. He cast him out. And during his temptation in the wilderness, he did not respond with dialogue. He simply replied with the words of Holy Scripture, with the Word of God. Be careful: the devil is a seducer. Never dialogue with him, because he is smarter than all of us and he will make us pay for it. When temptation arises, never dialogue. Close the door, close the window, close your heart. And in this way, we defend ourselves against this seduction, because the devil is astute. He is intelligent. He tried to tempt Jesus with quotes from the Bible, presenting himself as a great theologian. Be careful! One must not converse with

the devil, and we must not entertain ourselves with temptation. There is no dialogue. Temptation comes: we close the door. We keep watch over our heart.

Summing up, we all face numerous challenges in living a good life, but God will give us all the help we need to confront them and win out. All we need to do is struggle to correspond to God's grace. The very struggle will help us grow as human beings and make us more worthy of eternal life with God in heaven.

10

Encouraging others to go with us

When we consider the importance of the only goal that really matters in life – getting to heaven – and how few people there are who are aware of it and who actively pursue it, we naturally want to do all we can to help others follow this way. Often these others are members of our own family, colleagues of work, fellow members of clubs and societies to which we belong, or simply friends.

We can look at each one and ask ourselves: Does this person even know about life after death? Do they know there is a God and that God really loves them and wants them to be with him in heaven? Are they living the sort of life that will end in heaven? Do they know what is right and wrong, and are they truly sorry for their mistakes and sins?

If we asked these questions about our relatives and friends fifty years ago, the answer would have been very different from the answer today. Back then, far more people believed in God and belonged to some faith community. They were much better educated in morality, so that they knew what was right and wrong. In general, they were living better lives and were more firmly on the way to heaven. Today it is a very different story.

Concern for others' spiritual health

If we really care about our contemporaries – and we do, because we know them well and we want what is best for them – we will do all we can to help them in this most important area. If we see them losing weight and looking pale and without energy, we will ask them if they are well, and if they have seen a doctor. We care about their health, especially if we think they might have a serious illness. This is what friendship is.

Well then, if we are concerned about their bodily health, we will be even more concerned about their spiritual health. If we think that this is none of our business, that we can't bring up matters of religion with others because that is a private matter for each person, we immediately realise how foolish this reasoning is. Matters of religion are the most important question and, if we care about someone, we want to help them in what is most important.

St John Chrysostom, an early Christian bishop and saint, puts it very succinctly:

> When you discover something that has been of benefit to you, you make an effort to share it with others. You should therefore want others to accompany you along the pathways of the Lord. If you are going to the forum or to the baths and you come across someone who is idle, you invite him to accompany you. Apply this custom to the spiritual realm and, when you go to God, don't go alone (*Hom. In Evangelia*, VI, 6).

Everyone is looking for God

Another way to look at it is this. If we know something and we know that others would like to know it too, we will raise the question with them and explain it to them. Well, everyone is looking for God, whether they know it or not. How can we say this? Because every human being has an intellect and a will. The intellect, or mind, by its very nature seeks truth. It wants to know answers, especially to the most important questions. Questions like: Where did the universe come from? Has it always existed? What is the meaning of life? Is there life after death? Is there a God? The answer to all these questions is ultimately God.

And everyone has a will, which by nature seeks the good. When it finds a good it finds happiness. Depending on the value of the good, it will give more or less happiness. A good meal, a good book, an enjoyable holiday are all lesser goods which give a certain degree of happiness. But they can never satisfy the longing for true happiness, which everyone has. Even great wealth, or great fame, cannot do this. Only God, the infinite good, can. For this reason, St Augustine wrote in his *Confessions*, "Lord, you made us for you, and our heart is restless until it rests in you" (*Conf.* 1, 1, 1). We have seen evidence for this too in those who have had near-death experiences and have found themselves in heaven. They cannot begin to describe the level of their happiness there. It is greater than anything they have experienced on earth.

So, everyone is looking for God, and many people do not know it. We do. God needs us, our friends need us, to show them the way to the happiness they seek, the way to heaven. How are we going to do this? It is not difficult.

Example and word

The first step is giving good example. A person who believes in God and has a personal relationship with him naturally has more joy, more integrity, more peace, more concern for others. Others see this and they are drawn to it. They will often say: "I want what you have". There is something about a person who has faith that is very attractive. In a family or a workplace, such a person stands out, is different, is more caring, and others seek out that person for conversation, advice, or simply friendship. Inevitably they open up and talk about deeper matters. These can include how to be a better worker, spouse, parent, etc. And sooner or later, the question of God, the meaning of life, the goal of life, can come up. Example is all important and very effective.

Good example, as we have just seen, often leads to the next step, which is our word, our conversation. Those who think that you can't bring up matters of religion with others, because this is very personal and a taboo, should realise that this is nonsense. Where there is true friendship, others will naturally bring up these deeper matters, including religion, belief in God and belief in the next life. Often it will be the other person who is seeking answers who brings up these topics, but we can do it too. Always gently, with respect for the other person's privacy. We might say, for example, "I hope you don't mind my saying this, and please feel free not to answer, but you strike me as being a person with faith in God, or a person with some religious background". This can then lead to very deep and helpful conversations.

In the course of our conversation, we might also suggest that the person reads something we have found helpful: an article, a book, a YouTube clip… We can tell them why we found it useful and gently suggest that they look at it, giving them a copy whenever possible.

Also, we can invite them to a talk, a lecture, a day of reflection, a retreat, that we think might help them. Again, always gently, with respect for their freedom. We might offer to pick them up and drive them to the event. This will offer an opportunity to talk about it afterwards, to see how they took it and what they got out of it.

Instruments of God

And always, to pray very much for them. It will be God who moves them to come closer to him, not ourselves. We are only God's instruments. But important instruments, nonetheless. Often, without our intervention, those persons will not take that decisive step closer to God.

Pope St John Paul II spoke of the importance of this effort to a group of university students gathered in Rome from all over the world at Easter in 1982. He was speaking extemporaneously, not from prepared notes. In answer to something one of the students had said, he commented:

> Thinking about what you have said, there comes to mind a reflection that is probably related to my forthcoming trip to England. It is from an English writer – I think Cardinal Newman, although I am not sure – who, looking at London, a very large city which, like other large cities, easily becomes dechristianised, secularised, addressed this prayer to God: Give me ten saints and I will change this city. You students have spoken much about the bad spiritual situation of your contemporaries, who find themselves indifferent or uninterested, who don't feel any concern for spiritual, religious or ethical matters, who look on life superficially. I think that if this is true, the answer you can give is the one expressed in the prayer of which I have just spoken: give me ten saints and I will change this city. … In reality, everything is done through man. Certainly, man, if he allows himself to be led by the power of God, by the grace of God, if he walks close to God, is capable of

changing the world. This is my wish for you: that you improve the world.

Lest we be disheartened by the talk of being saints, to be a saint does not mean to be perfect. The saints were poor sinners too. But they were people of faith, of prayer, of concern for those around them. All this is within our grasp. And it will make all the difference.

Once again, St John Chrysostom encourages us in our effort to help others come closer to God:

> There is nothing colder than a Christian who is not concerned about the salvation of others... Do not say "I am unable to help them", for if you are truly a Christian it is impossible for you to make such an admission. The properties of natural things cannot be denied them: the same thing happens with this affirmation, for it is in the nature of a Christian to act in this way... It is easier for the sun to fail to give its light or its heat than for a Christian to cease to give light and warmth; it would be easier for light to be darkness. Do not say that the thing is impossible; what is impossible is the opposite. If we order our conduct aright, everything will follow as a natural consequence. The light of Christians cannot be hidden; a light that shines so brightly cannot be concealed (*Homilies on the Acts of the Apostles*, 20)

11

Sporting spirit

In a real way, our journey to heaven is very much like the quest of an athlete for success in sport. There are many common features and we do well to look at how athletes achieve their goals so that we can imitate them and achieve our more important goal.

Having a goal

It all starts with a goal. For the athlete, the goal may be to compete in the Olympic Games and possibly win a medal, or to be a national or state champion, or to be selected for the local team, or simply to get fit and enjoy the sport. So too, in our spiritual life, we have a goal, a very important one. Really, the most important one of all, before which any other goal in life is next to meaningless: to go to heaven when we die. Even if we won gold medals in the Olympics but didn't make it to heaven, our life will have been a total disaster – wasted.

So, just as the athlete always keeps the goal in mind, we should keep our heavenly goal very much in mind in our day-to-day decisions and actions. We should ask ourselves often whether the decision that we are now making, the activity that we are proposing to undertake, is going to help us achieve our goal or is rather going to be an obstacle to it. All our actions have a bearing, one way or another, on the achievement of the goal, and we should make sure they lead towards it.

St Paul wrote about this in several of his letters. He even compared the quest for sporting success with that for holiness of life. For example, in his first letter to his disciple Timothy he wrote:

> Train yourself in godliness; for while bodily training is of some value, godliness is of value in every way, as it holds promise for the present life and also for the life to come. The saying is sure and worthy of full acceptance. For to this end we toil and strive, because we have our hope set on the living God, who is the Saviour of all men, especially of those who believe (*1 Tim* 4:7-10).

Striving for the goal

Not only do athletes have a goal, but they earnestly strive to achieve it. They are determined to make it a reality. It means everything to them. It is their project, at least for the time being. They never leave it out of their sight. They dream of achieving it.

If they do that for the earthly goal of sporting success, what will we not do for the most important goal of all? We should remind ourselves often of the purpose and goal of our life. We were not created for life on earth, which lasts but a short time. We were created for eternal life with God in heaven. It is only natural to long for it and to keep it always in mind.

To go to heaven is to go home, to the house of the Father, as Jesus has told us. Spiritual writers have commented that when someone is away from home, he is eager to return there. He can't wait to get home. If we can't wait to get back to our earthly home, where we will live for our brief life on earth, how much more eager should we be to go home to heaven, where we will live for eternity.

Likewise, when we love someone dearly and we have been away from them for a long time, we can't wait to get back to see them, to give them a big hug and a kiss. So, as we grow here on earth in love for God, who is our Father and who has loved us with all our faults and has showered us with his graces, we can't wait to see him, and long to be with him in heaven.

Fifteen centuries ago, St Augustine wrote about the importance of this yearning to be with God in heaven:

> Our thoughts in this present life should turn on the praise of God, because it is in praising God that we shall rejoice for ever in the life to come; and no one can be ready for the next life unless he trains himself for it now. So we praise God during our earthly life, and at the same time we make our petitions to him. Our praise is expressed with joy, our petitions with yearning. We have been promised something we do not yet possess, and because the promise was made by one who keeps his word, we trust him and are glad; but insofar as possession is delayed, we can only long and yearn for it. It is good for us to persevere in longing until we receive what was promised, and yearning is over; then praise alone will remain (*Enarrationibus in psalmos*, Ps 148).

Various psalms in the Old Testament of the Bible express this longing. Among them are these two well-known ones:

> As a deer longs for flowing streams, so longs my soul for you, O God. My soul thirsts for God, for the living God. When shall I come and behold the face of God? (*Ps* 42:1-2).

> My heart says to you, "Your face, Lord, do I seek." Hide not your face from me (*Ps* 27:8-9).

We can learn a lot from these psalms and from athletes. It is not simply a matter of having a goal in the back of our mind and forgetting about it most of the time. We should keep it in the forefront of our thinking and earnestly strive to achieve it.

Sacrifice and self-control

It is no secret that every athlete who wants to achieve a lofty goal has to sacrifice other more enjoyable activities and comforts in order to achieve it. Often they will have a very demanding training regime. The athlete may complain to his trainer that it is too much, but if he wants to succeed in his sport, he follows it. Again, St Paul has something to say about it:

> Do you not know that in a race all the runners compete, but only one receives the prize? So run that you may obtain it. Every athlete exercises self-control in all things. They do it to receive a perishable wreath, but we an imperishable. Well, I do not run aimlessly, I do not box as one beating the air; but I pommel my body and subdue it, lest after preaching to others I myself should be disqualified (*1 Cor* 9:24-27).

We can learn a lot from this passage. First, there is a goal: to win the race, to receive the prize. But there is a difference with our own race. In a running race, only one person can come first and win the prize. In the race to heaven, everyone can be a winner. St Paul writes that God our Saviour "desires all men to be saved and to come to the knowledge of the truth" (*1 Tim* 2:4). Yes, God has a place in heaven for everyone, and it is up to us whether we occupy that place or not. If we fail, it won't be because God didn't want it, or because he didn't give us all the help we needed to obtain it.

Second, if we really want to go to heaven, we have to make the effort: "Run that you may obtain it". We must have the determination, the singlemindedness, to make the effort to live a good life and go to heaven. This is the most important goal anyone can have. Top athletes are determined to do well or they wouldn't have achieved the success they did. We too should have this determination, for a goal that is far more important than theirs. St Bernard of Clairvaux, a twelfth-century monk, urges us on in our quest for heaven. Thinking of the saints in heaven, who have already won the prize, he writes:

> Calling the saints to mind inspires, or rather arouses in us, above all else, a longing to enjoy their company, so desirable in itself. We long to share in the citizenship of heaven, to dwell with the spirits of the blessed, to join the assembly of patriarchs, the ranks of the prophets, the council of apostles, the great host of martyrs, the noble company of confessors and the choir of virgins. In short, we long to be united in happiness with all the saints. But our dispositions change. The Church of all the first followers of Christ awaits us, but we do nothing about it. The saints want us to be with them, and we are indifferent. The souls of the just await us, and we ignore them. Come brothers, let us at length spur ourselves on (*Sermon 2, Opera omnia*, Edit. Cisterc. 5, 1968).

Third, athletes live a spirit of sacrifice and self-control in all things. They may get up long before dawn to begin training, sacrificing more enjoyable activities during the day in order to train. It will often involve great effort, sometimes unpleasant effort. Consider the case of Czech tennis player, Ivan Lendl, widely regarded as one of the greatest tennis players of all time. After the Australian Open in 1988 he was interviewed about how he managed to hit the ball so hard. He answered that it was probably because of a weight-training program that had strengthened his upper body. He commented:

> I hate doing weights. I just absolutely hate it, and I have done quite a bit of it. I think it is extremely important for my game… Sometimes I come to the gym and I just sit there for 10 minutes and stare at those machines before I have the courage to start working. But it has to be done and I wish I had done it when I was 18, not 25.

Athletes also exercise self-control in matters of diet. They avoid certain foods which may make them put on weight, while eating other foods that will make them stronger or give them more energy. They may give up smoking or drinking alcohol. They may avoid staying out late at night, especially before a training session or a game. All of this will cost them, but they do it in order to achieve their goal.

In our spiritual life, we too need to sacrifice. This may involve little acts of self-denial, or mortifications, in matters like use of time, starting our work on time, doing the difficult jobs first, helping out at home, denying ourselves in food or drink, etc. Christ invited us to do this: "If any man would come after me, let him deny himself and take up his cross and follow me" (*Matt* 16:24). St Paul says that he did it too: "Well, I do not run aimlessly, I do not box as one beating the air; but I pommel my body and subdue it, lest after preaching to others I myself should be disqualified" (*1 Cor* 9:26-27).

A training program

Athletes always have a training program, usually set by the coach or trainer. It will involve hours of running, swimming, jumping, practising their sport, etc. Athletes are always trying to improve in specific ways. It may also involve hours in the gym, strengthening the muscles that are important for their particular sport. And generally these activities will be at the same time each day. We too, in our quest for eternal life, need a training program, a spiritual plan of life. It will involve regular times for spiritual activities each day.

Christians, especially Catholics, might consider the following plan, from which they can draw whatever they see as important at the present time. People of other faith traditions might have a very different plan. But it is important for everyone to have a plan with some set activities each day.

First thing in the morning, on getting out of bed, it is good to greet God and offer the whole day to him: our prayers, works, joys and sufferings, all for his glory. It is what we all the morning offering. This is a good time, too, to remind ourselves of why we are here on earth: to know, love and serve God, so that we may be happy with him forever in heaven. Reminding ourselves of the goal helps us order all our activities towards that end.

The morning may also be a good time to do some meditative prayer, talking with God in our own words. To do this, it might be necessary to rise early before the rest of the family gets up, in order to have peace and quiet. As our theme we might use the "book of life", some text of the Bible, or a passage from a spiritual book.

Our plan may involve attending Mass or some other spiritual activity on weekdays, as well as on Sundays.

It should include stopping at midday, or other times of the day, to say the Angelus, that traditional prayer that reminds us of how Mary the mother of Jesus, through her docility to the Holy Spirit, brought Jesus into the world.

It is always good too to say the rosary each day, meditating on the life of Christ as seen through the eyes of Mary.

And to do some spiritual reading, using one of the classics of centuries gone by or a good book by a modern writer, of which there are many.

At the end of the day, we do well to finish by saying a few prayers before we jump into bed. Often these will be prayers of thanksgiving for all the blessings of the day. At this time it can be very helpful too to do a brief examination of conscience, in which we look over the day while it is still fresh in our mind, and identify the good things we have done, and also our failings, for which we can say an act of sorrow with the intention of trying harder the next day.

Naturally, not everyone will be doing all these acts of piety. These are suggested so that each person can see what they are already doing, and what they might do in addition if they think it appropriate.

Our plan may also involve regular attendance at talks, seminars, retreats, etc., that can help us grow in the spiritual life.

The benefits of living an active life of prayer are enormous, far more than those of the sportsperson who has a demanding training routine. As St Paul says, athletes do it to win a perishable wreath, a laurel wreath in those days, whereas our prize is imperishable – eternal life with God in heaven. There is no comparison. It is worthwhile. But how determined are we, and to what lengths are we prepared to go, to ensure that we obtain the prize?

The coach

Every athlete that wants to succeed has a coach. The coach may not be as good as the athlete in that particular sport, but he or she knows enough about it to help the athlete. And the coach can watch the athlete and see things that the athlete does not. The coach also generally sets the training regime and pushes the athlete beyond their comfort zone.

Andre Agazzi, the great American tennis player, relates in his autobiography, Open, how his trainer Gil pushed him hard, to a point where he complained that he was getting tired. Gil replied: "I can't promise you that you won't be tired. But please know this. There's a lot of good waiting for you on the other side of tired. Get yourself tired, Andre. That's where you're going to know yourself. On the other side of tired."

The coach also helps the athlete focus on one particular aspect of the sport at a time, whichever aspect is most in need of improvement at that time. For example, in tennis it might be footwork, the grip, the serve, keeping the eye on the ball, etc. When this aspect has improved, they go on to another one, and so the athlete gradually improves.

All of this helps the athlete achieve goals beyond what they would have achieved without the coach. If athletes have a coach to help them compete for a crown that fades – a perishable wreath or a lot of money –, we too should have a coach in our spiritual athletics, where the prize is so much greater.

What sort of coach should we have? Really, it can be anyone who is struggling for holiness himself or herself, who has experience and has been at it longer than we have, who understands and lives the basics of the spiritual life, someone whom we trust and with whom we can relate well.

Sometimes the coach may be a priest or a religious man or woman. But it need not be. There are many lay people, including married ones, who are well versed in the spiritual life and who are struggling for holiness themselves, who can be a big help. Once we have found such a person, it is important that we see them regularly and that we open up to them about the realities, the successes and failures, we are experiencing. Regularity and sincerity are essential.

The spiritual coach will also help us focus our attention on one aspect of the spiritual life at a time, whichever aspect is most needed at that moment. It might be to spend more time in prayer, to be more patient, more orderly, more humble… We work on this aspect for a while, and when there has been some improvement, we go on to another one. In this way we make our way gradually up the inclined plane towards God.

Coping with failures

Along the way, athletes have to cope with failures, setbacks. Everyone has them. They may come in the form of injuries that take them out of action or even threaten their career altogether. Or they may be the normal failures that sportsmen and women experience from time to time: failing to win the important game or to perform at the level they expected, not winning the prize they were striving for… What do athletes do when that happens? They don't let it bother them. They pick themselves up, brush off the dust and get on with it, whether that means months of rehabilitation in the case of a serious injury, or simply regrouping mentally after a defeat. What they don't do is give up. The history of sport is filled with inspiring stories of people who suffered a serious injury and were told they would never play again, but who came back, sometimes better than before. Or others who went through a period of poor performance but who persevered and came back to their former glory.

Michael Jordan, one of the greatest basketball players of all time, looking back on his career, once commented:

> I've missed more than 9000 shots in my career. I've lost almost 300 games. Twenty-six times I've been trusted to take the game-winning shot and missed. I've failed over and over and over again in my life. And that is why I succeed.

One commentator said of Jordan: "He played every game as if it were his last". That is the way we should live too. Every day as if it were our last. One day it will be. And we may not know in advance which one. We could die today, for all we know. St James too, in his letter in the Bible, encourages us to live each day well:

> Come now, you who say: "Today or tomorrow we will go into such and such a town and spend a year there and trade and get gain"; whereas you do not know about tomorrow. What is your life? For you are a mist that appears for a little time and then vanishes. Instead you ought to say, "If the Lord wills, we shall live and we shall do this or that" (*James* 4:13-15).

In the spiritual life we may go through hard times too. It may be in the form of periods of dryness in which we get no joy out of prayer and even feel that God is just not there for us. Or we fall into a habit of serious sin, inclining us to stop struggling and to think we will never improve. If that happens, we may convince ourselves that the sin is not all that serious, or that there is no such thing as eternal life anyway. Or we just get slack and become lukewarm, praying less or not at all, indulging ourselves in food and drink, thinking too much about ourselves and forgetting about others ...

This can happen to anyone. But what we can't do is get discouraged and give up the struggle. If we give up, we make someone very happy. The devil. He is hell bent on getting us as far away from God as possible, and he will rejoice at yet another victory. It is then that we should remind ourselves of why we are here anyway. And that, as we have seen repeatedly, is to live a good life here on earth, with all the happiness that it brings, and then go to heaven with God forever. The alternative is hell, forever too. Take your pick.

No, like the athlete, we don't give up. We start over and strive to go back to the life we were living before, telling God we are sorry for our sins and asking his grace to do better in the future. This change may take some time, and it may involve the help of our spiritual coach, but what we can't do is stay down. There is too much at stake.

The doctor or physiotherapist

In addition to a coach, athletes will often have a doctor or physiotherapist. Athletes get injured from time to time and then they need their services. We too, in our spiritual struggle need their services. Obviously, we are not talking about physical injuries but spiritual ones: sins, spiritual lapses.

The doctor here is the priest or other minister, who can absolve our sins, restore our hope if we are getting discouraged, and give us spiritual advice about how to avoid falling in the future. The reality is that we are not perfect. We are frail and we do have falls. We need this help, and we should have some minister to whom we can go, preferably someone who knows us well. Yes, we could go to any minister, but we all understand that the one who knows us best can help us more. After all, we don't take our body to a different doctor each time, our car to a different mechanic, or our teeth to a different dentist. Let us be honest and take our soul to a priest who knows us. If confession is available in our religious group, we can avail ourselves of this very helpful practice to be forgiven by God and start over.

Following the rules

Every sport has its rules. In some cases, the rulebook is very thick, with all the eventualities listed and the penalties for infringement laid out. In other cases it may be very thin. But every sport has rules. Athletes know they must follow the rules or incur the penalty. St Paul writes to Timothy: "An athlete is not crowned unless he competes according to the rules" (*2 Tim* 2:5).

The game of life has rules too. They can be summarised in the Ten Commandments given by God to Moses on Mount Sinai. We all have a general sense of what they are, but we do well to read up on them from time to time, especially if we have any doubts about particular moral issues. And we can ask someone who knows them well to clarify them for us. We don't want to appear before God in the judgment and be found ignorant of something we should have known. There are some areas, especially as regards the natural law, where ignorance is no excuse. The *Catechism of the Catholic Church* and my book *The Final Exam – Preparing for the Judgment*, which is based on the Catechism and explains it in simple terms, can be helpful in this regard.

As we are well aware, and we have considered it numerous times, we are not perfect. We don't always succeed in obeying God's laws, as hard as we try. We are poor human beings, sinners. All of us. God understands that. He made us, and he knows the weaknesses of our human nature. For that reason, when we fail to follow the rules of life, the moral law, we should be sorry and resolve to try harder in the future. And we should remember the joy that following the rules always gives us.

We should always remember what the *Catechism of the Catholic Church* teaches as regards those who are not sorry for serious sins: "To die in mortal sin without repenting and accepting God's merciful love means remaining separated from him for ever by our own free choice. This state of definitive self-exclusion from communion with God and the blessed is called 'hell'" (*CCC*, n. 1033). This applies to people of all religious beliefs, not just to Christians. It would be tragic indeed if, after setting out earnestly on the road to eternal life in heaven, we were not sorry for a serious sin and thus missed out on the goal altogether. And, of course, if we ended up suffering the pains of hell for all eternity.

Time-outs

Many team sports have time-outs, or at least quarter-time or half-time breaks. Here the team gathers to catch their breath and to consider how they are going and what strategy they should follow in the next period.

In the spiritual life we need time-outs too. Times in which we can look back at how we have gone and how we can improve. They are very important. Without them, we will tend to continue doing the same things and at the same pace as before. This may not be good enough. Naturally, our spiritual coach can help us see how we need to improve and how we can go about it. But as individuals we need times to reflect on how we are following the advice of our coach, how we have gone in the past, and what we can change in order to do better.

These time-outs often take the form of monthly pauses for prayer in what are sometimes called days of recollection. Here we take time to reflect on how we are going and how we can improve, often assisted by someone who guides us. But here we have to be careful. The tendency will always be to think that we are too busy to stop and pray, that we don't have time for this. Or that we really don't need to do this, because we are going pretty well as it is. Then we can easily slip back into lukewarmness and not proceed at the pace God wants for us.

We benefit too from longer, yearly, periods of reflection, often called retreats. We can do them on our own, but it is always better to attend a retreat, if available, where someone else gives the input. In these we can look back at the whole year, see how we have gone over this longer period of time, and make resolutions to centre our struggle for the coming year.

These periods of reflection are extremely beneficial in helping us move forward and upward. And not stagnate, remaining in the same place or going at a sluggish pace.

Finishing the race

As is obvious, it is not enough to know the goal of life and set off to obtain it. We must run the race to the end. We cannot give up because it is too hard. Yes, life may be difficult at times, and we can be sorely tempted to give up. This can happen if we suffer considerable adversity, like a serious illness, the death of a loved one, the loss of a job, the loss of our good reputation through the lies of others ... But we know that God is always there for us, that he loves us and he invites us to come closer to him. Jesus says: "Come to me, all who labour and are heavy laden, and I will give you rest. Take my yoke upon you and learn from me; for I am gentle and lowly in heart, and you will find rest for your souls. For my yoke is easy and my burden is light" (*Matt* 11:28).

Jesus Christ suffered too, more than we ever will, but he carried his cross to the end and died on it so that we might have life, eternal life. He is always there to accompany us along the way. He entered the world of suffering on becoming man, and he is here with us, especially if we are going through hard times. And we should never forget that after his cross came the resurrection. The same will happen to us. There may be crosses in life but they will be followed by our own resurrection to eternal life. And the more we have suffered, the greater the reward will be.

We must not give up. We must continue until the end, as athletes do. There are well-known instances in which a marathon runner suffered cramps and fell several times toward the end of the race, but got up each time and finished the race, sometimes long after the previous runner. He or she was met with the admiration and applause of the spectators. Our sport is far more important than theirs. We too must finish the race.

We take heart from St Paul, who suffered so much for his faith and for sharing it with others. He came to the end of his life in a Roman prison and, knowing that he had little time left to live, wrote to his disciple Timothy: "I am already on the point of being sacrificed; the time of my departure has come. I have fought the good fight, I have finished the race, I have kept the faith. From now on there is laid up for me the crown of righteousness which the Lord, the righteous judge, will award to me on that Day, and not only to me but also to all who have loved his appearing" (2 Tim 4:6-8).

Yes, it is a great joy to finish the race of life, to come to the end of our journey, and then be welcomed home to the Father's house. To pass from time here on earth to eternity with God in heaven. Then we will hear those welcome words, "Well done, good and faithful servant; you have been faithful over a little, I will set you over much; enter into the joy of your master" (*Matt* 25:23).

www.ingramcontent.com/pod-product-compliance
Lightning Source LLC
Chambersburg PA
CBHW050553160426
43199CB00015B/2648